Beaded Elegance

HOME ACCENTS AND GIFTS TO MAKE

Martingale®
& COMPANY

Beaded Elegance: Home Accents and Gifts to Make
© 2004 by Martingale & Company®

Martingale & Company
20205 144th Avenue NE
Woodinville, WA 98072-8478
www.martingale-pub.com

Printed in China
09 08 07 06 05 04   8 7 6 5 4 3 2 1

Library of Congress Cataloging-in-Publication Data
Beaded elegance / compiled by Dawn Anderson.
    p. cm.
  ISBN 1-56477-515-1
 1. Beadwork. I. Anderson, Dawn
  TT860.B3339 2004
  745.58'2--dc22

2003021719

Credits

President • Nancy J. Martin
CEO • Daniel J. Martin
Publisher • Jane Hamada
Editorial Director • Mary V. Green
Managing Editor • Tina Cook
Technical Editor • Dawn Anderson
Copy Editor • Karen Koll
Illustrators • Laurel Strand and Robin Strobel
Design Director • Stan Green
Cover and Text Designer • Shelly Garrison
Photographer • Bill Lindner
Photo Stylist • Bridget Haugh
Photo Assistant • Jason Lund

Mission Statement
Dedicated to providing quality products and service to inspire creativity.

Contents

Introduction

They sparkle and shimmer, glitter and glimmer. They catch the sunlight and glow at twilight. There are hundreds of styles to choose from and even more ways to enjoy them. They're beautiful beads!

Beaded home accents are popping up in stores across the country. With a handful of beads and a few simple tools, you can quickly transform a plain-Jane item into something undeniably unique. An infinite selection of sizes, shapes, and colors of beads—and the elegant designs in *Beaded Elegance*—make it possible.

Most of the projects within these pages are so simple, they come together in just a few short steps. Create a cascade of beads on a lamp-shade. Add a romantic twinkle to a candle setting. Grace a bed or sofa with exotic beaded pillows. Fleck a fabric-covered frame with amber glass beads. Swag strings of sapphire from a chandelier, fringe a table runner, and stitch gorgeous beaded place mats for a night of extra-special dining. Shower holiday ornaments with hundreds of tiny seed beads. Combine beads with wire, fabric, thread, glass, or metal for a variety of eye-catching results.

Whatever beads you choose—crystal, metal, fire-polished, fiber optic, pressed glass, ceramic, transparent, iridescent (even bells, pendants, and charms)—you'll enjoy endless creativity with speedy results. You can have something spectacular to show off in a few hours or less. Let's get started!

Getting Started

Beads

Beads are available in an almost infinite range of sizes, shapes, colors, and materials. Many of the projects in this book are created with seed beads, which are available in a wide assortment of colors and in a variety of finishes including transparent, rainbow, opaque, silver-lined, and iridescent. Size 11 seed beads are the most frequently used. They are often sold in vials, hanks (12 lengths of pre-strung beads, each about 20" long), or bags. Although a project may call for size 11 seed beads on a hank, you can easily substitute seed beads sold in a vial or bag as long as they are the same size. Size 6 seed beads (also called pony beads) are used for some of the projects in this book. The smaller the number of the bead size, the larger it is, so a size 6 seed bead is larger than a size 11 seed bead. Bugle beads are also frequently used in beaded projects. These beads are narrow tubes typically about 2 mm in diameter in a variety of lengths. Many other kinds of beads are incorporated into the projects in this book as well, but are generally used in smaller quantities for accent or embellishment.

Beaded Trims

You can find an assortment of pre-beaded trims available at many fabric and craft stores. These can be used to create beaded projects quickly and with little time investment. Beaded fringes are available in many colors and lengths and are usually attached to a ribbon heading. The ribbon is typically sewn into the seam of a project as was done on the Turkish Table Runner on page 33. Or it can be glued to a project and concealed with a second trim as shown on the Floral Lampshade on page 7. Both of these projects also incorporate beaded appliqués. You can purchase appliqués individually or cut them from beaded lace yardage.

Wire

Most of the bead and wire projects in this book were strung on spool wire in the three basic metal colors of silver, gold, and copper. Spool wire is generally available in sizes from 20 to 32 gauge. The larger the gauge number, the smaller the diameter of the wire. Most often, 28-gauge wire is used for stringing size 11 seed beads. You can also find a wide range of packaged wire in coils, in a variety of gauges, in craft and hardware stores, including permanently colored copper wire. Sterling silver wire was used to make the frame for the Sparkling Vase on page 61 and is sold by the foot at specialty bead stores (see "Sources" on page 80). You could substitute less-expensive copper wire for the frame of the vase. Copper is a softer metal, however, and doesn't hold its shape as readily. Brass rods (see "Sources" on page 80) were used to create the wire frame for the ornaments on page 37. The rods are quite inexpensive and are rigid, so they hold their shape well, preventing distortion of the finished ornament. For best results, choose a color of wire that coordinates with your beads or matches the wire frame you are beading around. For example, packaged black craft wire was used for the Crystal-Draped Chandelier on page 49 to match the wire color to the black finish on the chandelier.

Findings

Eye pins: These pins consist of a long piece of wire with a loop at one end. They are used for holding one or more beads to create a beaded drop. Adding a second loop on the other end of a beaded eye pin allows you to connect beads to make a beaded chain or garland.

Head pins: These pins resemble long skinny nails with blunt ends. They are used for holding one or more beads to create a beaded drop.

Jump rings: These are metal rings that can be pried open and connected to other metal rings or wire frames to join pieces together.

Tools and Supplies

Beading needle: A thin needle with a sharp tip used for stitching beads to fabric. Size 12 is suitable for most beaded embroidery projects.

Beading thread: A special thread used for sewing beads to fabric. It is available in waxed and unwaxed varieties. Unwaxed beading thread can be waxed with beeswax to help prevent fraying.

Chain-nose pliers: These pliers are flat and smooth on the inside of the jaws and have pointed ends. They are used to grab wire in tight places and for twisting wire ends together.

Flat-nose pliers: These pliers are flat and smooth on the inside of the jaws, but have a wide end that is squared off. These pliers work well for bending angles in wire.

Glue: Fabri-Tac Permanent Adhesive can be used to bond beaded appliqués, beads, and trims to fabric surfaces. It is solvent based and dries rapidly, so it is important to work quickly.

Mandrel: This is an instrument around which wire can be shaped. Wire can be wrapped around something as simple as a dowel, knitting needle, or nail. Simply look for something that has the diameter you need.

Round-nose pliers: These pliers have rounded jaws and taper at the tip. They are used for shaping wire into loops, such as on an eye pin or at the center of a coil. Because the diameter is larger at the interior of the jaws and tapers at the tip, you can create loops of different sizes by adjusting where you position the wire along the length of the jaws.

Wire cutters: Many cutters make angled cuts. For best results use a flush cutter. This kind of cutter makes a straight cut on one piece of the cut wire and an angled cut on the other piece. You want to have straight cuts, so you may need to flip the cutter and recut the other piece of wire to get a flush cut on the ends of both pieces. A larger cutter will be better for cutting thicker wires.

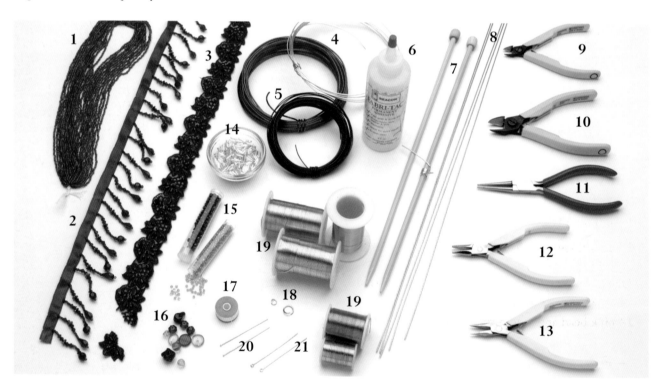

1. Prestrung seed breads	8. Brass rods	15. Seed beads in vials
2. Beaded fringe	9. Small wire cutters	16. Assorted accent beads
3. Beaded lace (cut apart to make appliqués)	10. Large wire cutters	17. Beading thread
4. Sterling silver wire	11. Round-nose pliers	18. Jump rings
5. Coiled craft wire	12. Flat-nose pliers	19. Spool wire
6. Adhesive	13. Chain-nose pliers	20. Head pins
7. Knitting needles used as mandrels	14. Bugle beads	21. Eye pins

Beaded rose appliqués combined with pink beaded fringe and delicate sequin rosette trim transform a plain pink lampshade into a whimsical decorative showpiece—and only a little gluing is required!

The lampshade I used was divided into six separate panels, making it easy to create one pattern that could be repeated on each panel. I loved these pink rose appliqués, but glued pearlescent seafoam green sequins over the bright green leaves so that the appliqués would better match the soft color palette I desired. To add detail to the background, I created "dots" by layering a flat green sequin over a larger pink one. Then I glued the layered sequins in rows over the background of each panel. I finished the shade by gluing pre-beaded fringe to the lower edge, and then applying a sequin rosette trim over the fringe heading and along the upper edge of the shade.

Floral Lampshade

By Genevieve A. Sterbenz

Materials

- Light pink silk fabric lampshade
- One 6" length of 5-mm-wide prestrung sequins in pearlescent pink
- One 6" length of 4-mm-wide prestrung sequins in pearlescent seafoam green
- 24 pink bead and sequin rose appliqués, 1" wide
- 1 yard of prestrung pink beaded fringe
- 1½ yards of pale pink sequin rosette trim
- Scissors
- 2 small bowls to hold loose sequins
- Ruler
- Tweezers
- Fabri-Tac Permanent Adhesive (see "Sources" on page 80)

Instructions

1. Place lampshade on clean, flat work surface. Cut the string on the prestrung length of pink sequins and slide sequins off string into bowl. In a second bowl, repeat for green sequins. Using the placement diagram below right as a guide, turn lampshade on its side and use tweezers to position rows of pink sequins and four rose sequin appliqués on one panel of the lampshade. Measure distance between sequins and rows and adjust spacing as desired.

2. When comfortable with the placement, use tweezers to lift one pink sequin, add a dab of glue to the underside and return to its original position. Repeat for all the remaining pink sequins. Then, add a dab of glue to the underside of one green sequin and use tweezers to center and adhere on top of one pink sequin. Repeat, adding green sequins to all the remaining pink sequins. When all rows are completed, secure rose appliqués in place with glue to complete the first panel. Repeat in the same manner on the remaining five panels of the shade.

   Note: I glued flat green sequins to the leaves of my appliqués before securing them in place.

DESIGNER'S TIP

The glue used in this project dries fast. Handle sequins with tweezers and work quickly for the best results.

3. Place the cut end of the fringe heading (ribbon that the fringe is stitched to) at the back seam of the lampshade along the bottom edge, making sure that all beads hang below the bottom edge of the lampshade. Add a dab of glue on the underside of the fringe heading; press down to adhere. My lampshade had a self-fabric bias trim strip around the upper and lower edges of the shade, and I glued the fringe heading right over the existing self-fabric trim. Continue adding glue and pressing fringe heading down around the entire bottom edge of the lampshade. Cut fringe heading at the back seam where the ends meet, trimming away excess.

4. Beginning again at the back seam along the bottom edge, apply dabs of glue to the back of the rosette trim and secure over the ribbon heading of the fringe along the entire bottom edge of the lampshade. Cut the trim at the back seam where ends meet. To apply sequin rosette trim around the top of the lampshade, begin at the back seam along the top edge and secure end to upper edge with glue. Continue gluing trim around upper edge of lampshade. Cut the trim at the back seam where ends meet.

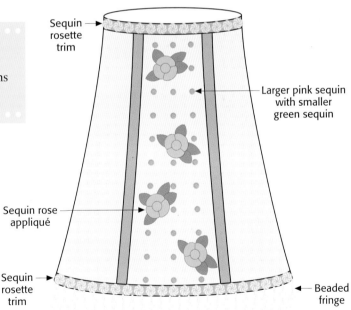

Sequin rosette trim

Larger pink sequin with smaller green sequin

Sequin rose appliqué

Sequin rosette trim

Beaded fringe

Placement Diagram

This exquisite beaded flower looks more complex than it is. It can be created in just a few short steps. All the petals and the leaf are made individually using the same technique. They all have wire stems, which are gathered up and wrapped around a bead-covered metal ring. The ring becomes the flower's "stem."

Flower Napkin Ring

By Natalie Norman

Materials
(for 1 napkin ring)

- 2 packages of size 11 iridescent light fuchsia seed beads for outer flower petals
- 1 package of size 11 iridescent light orchid seed beads for inner flower petals
- One 4" vial of size 11 celery seed beads for leaf
- One 4" vial of size 11 light green seed beads for stem
- One 4" vial of size 11 yellow seed beads for stamens
- 3 size 6 gold seed beads for stamens
- 28-gauge silver-colored spool wire
- 1⅞"-diameter gold metal ring
- Shallow dish
- Wire cutters
- Chain-nose pliers

Instructions

1. Pour beads for outer petals into shallow dish. Thread about 13" of seed beads onto spool wire. Without cutting wire from spool, make a loop with 12" of wire, twisting end around main wire to secure. This loop will become the stem.

2. Push seven beads down as far as you can and separate from remaining beads on the spool wire. Make another loop just above the seven beads with 5" of wire and twist to secure so the seven beads fit tightly between the two wire loops.

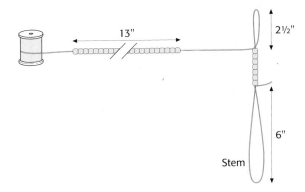

3. Push down 8 or 9 beads and wrap the length of beads around the left side of the row of seven beads. Wrap wire around the long wire loop.

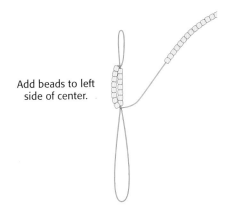

Add beads to left side of center.

4. Push down 9 or 10 more beads and wrap around the remaining (right) side of the seven beads, wrapping once around the short loop to secure. This completes one row around the petal center. Continue to add rows of beads around the 7 center beads, increasing the number of beads with each row as necessary until you have added a total of six rows to the left of the 7 center beads of the petal.

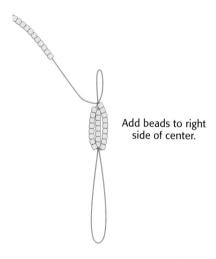

Add beads to right side of center.

5. Wrap wire several times around the stem to secure and then trim off excess, cutting wire from spool.

6. Cut off the top loop of wire leaving ¼" and fold the bare wires to the back of the petal. Make a total of six outer flower petals. Repeat process to make one leaf using the celery beads, but start with nine beads in the center rather than seven to make the leaf slightly longer than the outer petals.

7. Pour light orchid beads into a clean shallow dish. Thread about 5½" of beads onto spool wire. Make five inner flower petals in the same manner as the outer flower petals, starting with four beads for the center and continuing to add rows of beads until there are four rows on the left side of the petal.

8. Cut a piece of wire 8" long. Thread a size 6 bead onto the wire, fold wire in half around the bead, and twist just under the bead to secure it in place. Thread nine size 11 beads onto both wires and push them up under the larger bead. Thread one bead onto one of the wires and twist both wires under it to secure. Repeat to make a total of three stamens.

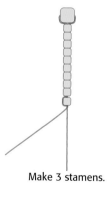

Make 3 stamens.

9. Arrange the stamens inside inner petals; surround by outer petals and hold like a bouquet. Twist the wires around the base of the flower a couple times to hold everything in place. Set aside.

10. Thread about 3' of wire with the stem beads. Wrap the beaded wire around the metal ring and twist to secure. Continue wrapping the wire around the ring, pushing the beads up as you go. Continue making wraps around the ring, pushing the rows tightly together to conceal the metal ring. When you reach the end, trim wire from the spool, leaving a 3" tail. Insert the end into the holes of the first ring of beads. Then twist the two ends together for ⅜" and trim off excess. Push ends between rows of beds.

11. Wrap wires from flower and leaf around beaded metal ring, and then wrap wires around base of flower to secure in place.

Elegant embroidered fabric served as the inspiration for the beaded accents added to this diminutive box. Fabric, glue, seed beads, and a premade tassel transformed the plain wooden box into something beautiful.

To cover the exterior of the box, I selected an embroidered fabric so that I could use it as a guide for the beading. I chose seed beads that closely matched the flower colors to further enhance the existing pattern.

Silk Box

By Genevieve A. Sterbenz

Materials

Note: The materials listed below are for a 4½" x 4½" x 3" box. If you use a different size box, fabric yardages and bead requirements may also change. See instructions for fabric calculations.

- 4½" x 4½" x 3" tall wood box
- 4½" x 4½" square of batting
- ¼ yard of fabric with embroidered pattern for outside of box
- ¼ yard of lining fabric for interior of box
- Beaded tassel, about 2¼" long
- 1 hank of size 11 seed beads for each flower color in the fabric
- 15-mm bead for tassel accent
- Newspaper
- Ruler
- Scissors
- Spray adhesive
- Thin cardboard
- Table knife
- Awl
- Masking tape
- Contact cement
- Fabri-Tac Permanent Adhesive
- Small bowls
- Tweezers

DESIGNER'S TIP

The following instructions for creating a fabric-covered box are for any size or shape box, fitting the following description: The box needs to have a lid that has some depth to it, is flush with the rest of the box, and can be completely removed from the base of the box. This is not as complicated as it may sound. A recipe file box is a perfect example of the type of box you need. If you find a wooden box that fits the description above, yet is already hinged, you can very easily remove the hinges with a small pair of pliers so that you can separate the lid from the base.

Instructions
(for a box of any size)

1. Place box on clean, flat work surface. Separate the lid from the bottom of the box, setting the bottom aside. Cover a second and third work surface with newspaper. The newspaper will need to be replenished often. Measure, mark, and cut a piece of batting equal to the surface area of the top of the lid (A = total length of batting; B = total width of batting). Set batting aside. Measure, mark, and cut a piece of embroidered fabric that will cover the top of the lid completely and the sides of the box partially. (Use this formula: A + C = total length of fabric; B + C = total width of fabric.)

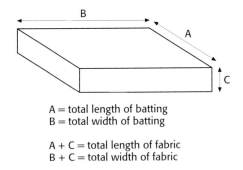

A = total length of batting
B = total width of batting

A + C = total length of fabric
B + C = total width of fabric

2. Place lid, right side up, on newspaper. Apply light coat of spray adhesive to top and sides. Position batting on top of lid and press down to adhere. Apply another light coat of spray adhesive to the batting. Move lid to clean newspaper. Center fabric over top of lid and press outside edges of fabric to the sides of the lid and smooth flat. Fold in excess at corners along the sides of the box and glue in place. Set lid aside.

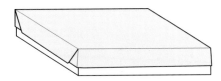

3. Measure, mark, and cut a piece of cardboard equal to the length and width of three sides of the lid (2A + B = total length of cardboard; C = total width of piece of cardboard). Score the cardboard as shown with the dull edge of a table knife. Set the cardboard aside. Measure, mark, and cut a piece of embroidered fabric that is 1" longer and four times wider than the cardboard (2A + B + 1" = total length of fabric; 4C = total width of fabric).

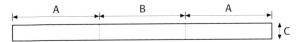

2A + B = total length of piece of cardboard
C = total width of piece of cardboard
2A + B + 1" = total length of fabric
4C = total width of fabric

Place fabric, wrong side up, on clean newspaper. Apply light thin coat of spray adhesive. Transfer fabric to clean work surface. Place cardboard strip, scored side down, lengthwise near top of fabric, leaving ¼" above strip and ½" on each side.

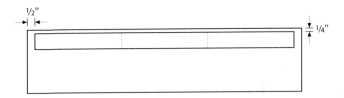

Fold top ¼" of fabric over and adhere to cardboard. Fold entire cardboard strip over again. Smooth flat to adhere. Using an awl, make a small hole through the cardboard and fabric, in the center of the cardboard strip. Lift the fabric-covered cardboard strip slightly to feed the ribbon of the beaded tassel through the hole. Pull the ribbon through to the back side, which is the side that is face up. Pull ribbon taut and flatten it to the side of the hole. Secure in place with a piece of tape.

4. Return entire piece (wrong side up) to clean newspaper and apply another coat of spray adhesive. Bring the fabric-covered cardboard band to the lid. Gently fold at the scored marks. Center the front piece with the tassel on the front side of the lid. Press to adhere, letting the rest of the fabric hang

down below. Wrap the two side pieces around the lid, and the ½" of extra fabric on each side onto the back of the lid.

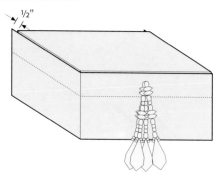

Front of lid

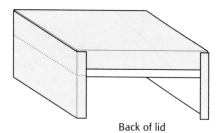

Back of lid

5. Turn the lid over and press the remaining fabric on two opposite sides onto the interior sides and bottom of the lid. Repeat with the remaining side, clipping at corners as necessary. Use dabs of contact cement if necessary.

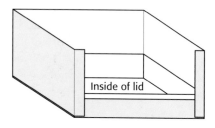

Inside of lid

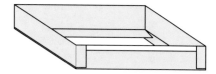

6. Measure, mark, and cut a piece of cardboard equal to the surface area of the inside of the lid (E = total length of cardboard; F = total width of cardboard). Set cardboard aside. Measure, mark, and cut a piece of lining fabric that is 1" longer and 1" wider than the cardboard (E + 1" = total length of fabric; F + 1" = total width of fabric). Place fabric wrong side up on clean newspaper and apply light coat of spray adhesive. Transfer fabric to clean work surface. Center cardboard over fabric and press down to adhere. Fold up two opposite sides of fabric and secure to cardboard. Repeat with remaining opposite sides. Use dabs of contact cement to secure corners. Set aside.

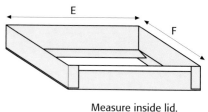

Measure inside lid.

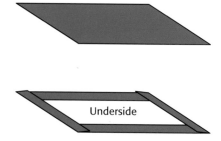

Underside

7. Measure, mark, and cut a piece of embroidered fabric 1" longer than the length of three sides, and 2" longer than the depth of the box (2A + B + 1" = total length of fabric needed; D + 2" = total width of fabric needed).

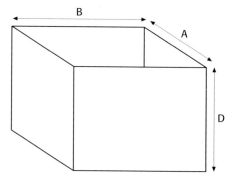

2A + B + 1" = length of fabric needed
D + 2" = width of fabric needed

Place fabric wrong side up on clean newspaper and apply light coat of spray adhesive. Transfer fabric to clean work surface. Cover three sides of the box by positioning the fabric so that 1" of extra fabric extends above and below the box and ½" of fabric wraps around each corner on the fourth side.

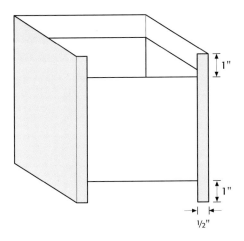

Press excess fabric on two opposite sides into the inside and onto the bottom of the box. Smooth flat to secure. Repeat to wrap excess fabric to the inside and bottom on the remaining sides. Use dabs of contact cement if necessary.

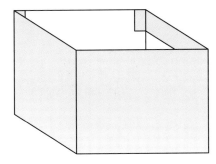

8. Referring to the illustration in step 7 on page 16, measure, mark, and cut a piece of embroidered fabric to create the inside hinge between the box and lid (D = total length of fabric needed; B = total width of fabric needed). Place fabric wrong side up on clean newspaper and apply light coat of spray adhesive. Place bottom of box with the front side facing forward on work surface. Position fabric

right side up at the back interior of the box so that the bottom ½" to ¾" of the fabric adheres to the box, leaving the remaining fabric free.

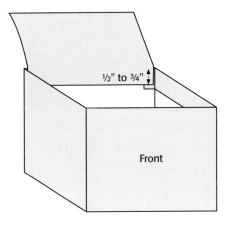

Then, place the lid in the "up" position, matching the back edges of the box and lid. Press the remaining fabric into the interior of the lid along the side and top. Close the box to make sure that all sides line up evenly. The fabric hinge can be removed and repositioned once or twice if necessary. The hinge should be slightly loose so that the lid can move easily.

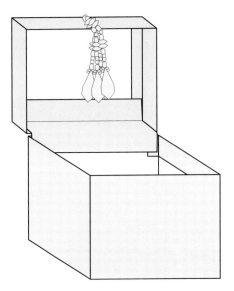

9. Place box with back side facing up on clean work surface. Referring to the illustrations on page 18, measure, mark, and cut a piece of cardboard equal to the surface area of the back side of the box with

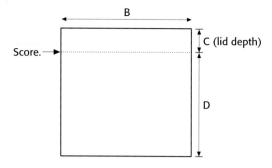

the lid closed (C + D = total length of cardboard needed; B = total width of cardboard needed). Score cardboard as shown. Set cardboard aside.

Measure, mark, and cut a piece of embroidered fabric 2" longer and 1" wider than the cardboard (C + D + 2" = total length of fabric needed; B + 1" = total width of fabric needed). Place fabric wrong side up on clean newspaper and apply light coat of spray adhesive. Transfer fabric to clean work surface. Position cardboard on fabric as shown.

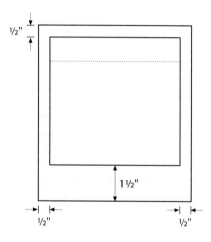

Fold over opposite long sides and smooth flat. Apply dabs of contact cement on top corners, fold over excess fabric at top, and smooth flat with hands.

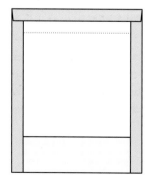

In same position, transfer fabric-covered cardboard to clean newspaper and apply spray adhesive. Position against back side of box, with edges even and scored line at joint between lid and base. Wrap remaining bottom piece of fabric around the bottom edge and smooth flat on bottom of box. Set box aside.

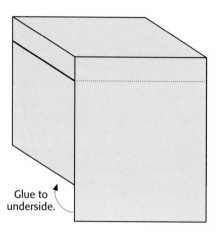

Glue to underside.

10. Measure, mark and cut two pieces of cardboard equal to the surface area of the inside of the box in the same manner as for the box lid in step 6 on page 16. Cover each piece with fabric as in step 6. One piece will be used for the bottom interior and one piece will be used to cover the bottom exterior of the box. Set aside both pieces.

11. Measure, mark and cut a piece of cardboard based on the interior measurements of the box bottom (G + H + I + J = total length of cardboard needed; K + ¼" = total width of cardboard needed).

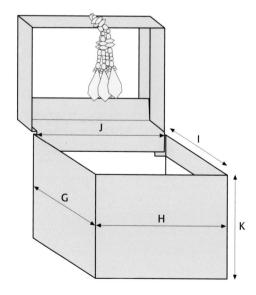

Score the cardboard according to the illustration. Set aside.

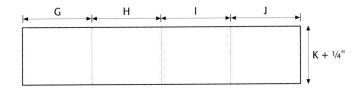

Measure, mark, and cut a piece of coordinating solid fabric 2" longer and 2¼" wider than the cardboard (G + H + I + J + 2" = total length of lining fabric needed; K + 2¼" = total width of lining needed). Place fabric on clean newspaper and apply light coat of spray adhesive. Transfer fabric to clean work surface, keeping adhesive side up. Center cardboard on fabric scored side down.

Bring up opposite long sides and fold them over onto cardboard and smooth flat. Fold in the corners on one side and then using scissors, trim out excess fabric and discard. Use dabs of contact cement to secure corners. Repeat with opposite side. Turn fabric-covered cardboard to right side and fold at each scored line. Set aside interior-wall piece.

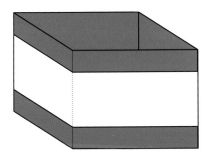

Fold interior-wall piece on scored lines.

12. Place both top and bottom interior pieces and bottom exterior piece wrong sides up on clean newspaper and apply spray adhesive. Place lid interior piece inside lid and press to secure. Place bottom interior piece inside bottom of box and press to secure. Turn box upside down and place bottom exterior piece on bottom of box; press to secure. Set box right side up and open lid. Brush contact cement on interior walls of box. Then slip folded, fabric-covered, interior-wall piece into the box, wrong sides together. Hold in place for a short time to secure.

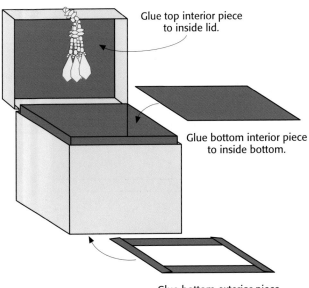

Glue top interior piece to inside lid.

Glue bottom interior piece to inside bottom.

Glue bottom exterior piece to outside bottom.

13. Cut the string on the prestrung length of one color of seed beads and slide beads off string into bowl. Repeat for each remaining string of beads, putting each color of beads into a separate bowl. Choose one flower or piece of the pattern that you desire to bead. Apply dabs of glue, keeping within the lines. Using tweezers, apply beads to the glued area. Continue to add glue and beads until the desired effect is reached. Do one side at a time and allow for drying time in between. Repeat on all sides of the box.

14. To add the larger bead at the tassel, turn the box so that the front is facing upward. Add a dab of glue at the top of the tassel and place bead using tweezers. Let dry.

Beaded tassels and fringe can give an elegant look to otherwise plain pillows. I chose to make my own tassels and fringe for these pillows rather than use prebeaded fringe or ready-made tassels. This provided me with an almost endless range of bead colors to choose from for a more custom color match. These pillows are simple to make; however, you can also add beaded tassels to ready-made pillows.

Pillows with Tassels and Fringe

By Carol Pilot

Materials

(for pillow with fringe)

- ½ yard of blue velveteen
- ¼ yard of blue brocade
- ½ yard of flat silver trim, ⅜" wide
- One 6" vial of size 11 blue seed beads
- 1 package of size 6 silver-lined crystal seed beads
- About 70 blue beads, 6 x 9 mm
- Blue and gray sewing thread
- Gray beading thread and beading needle
- 12" x 16" pillow form
- General sewing supplies:
  - Sewing machine
  - Iron and ironing board
  - Rotary cutter, ruler, and self-healing cutting mat
  - Marking pencil
  - Scissors
  - Straight pins
  - Hand-sewing needle

Instructions

1. Press fabrics; press velveteen from the wrong side. Cut two 13" x 17" rectangles from velveteen and one 5" x 17" rectangle from brocade. Mark a line on the front of one rectangle of velveteen 4" from

one long side. Position brocade wrong side down over center of marked rectangle, aligning one long edge of brocade with the marked line. Stitch through both layers ½" from marked line. Fold brocade fabric over and press. Align edges of brocade with edges of velveteen and baste ⅜" from all edges.

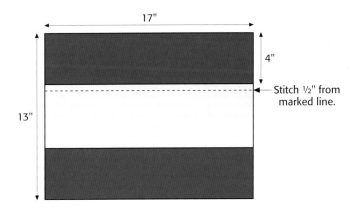

Stitch ½" from marked line.

Baste brocade ⅜" from raw edges.

2. Center flat silver trim over seam line; pin. Stitch on both sides of trim with gray thread.

Stitch close to both edges of trim.

3. Mark points along the edges of the velveteen rectangles, ¼" and 3" from corners. Align ruler with ¼" mark on one side of fabric and 3" mark on adjacent side of fabric. Trim, using rotary cutter. Repeat on each side of each corner to taper corners slightly. Repeat on remaining rectangle.

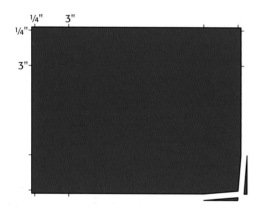

4. Pin velveteen rectangles, right sides together. Stitch ½" from raw edges, leaving an opening for turning. Trim corners. Turn cover right side out.

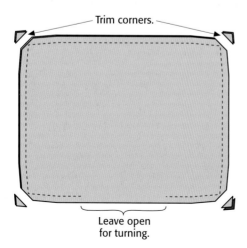

Trim corners.

Leave open for turning.

5. Thread beading needle with single strand of beading thread, about 30" long. Secure thread to seam allowance on inside of pillow, next to silver trim. Take a stitch through cover to front side, exiting at the lower edge of the silver trim at the side seam allowance. Thread beads onto needle in the order shown to make first length of fringe (the longer length). At last seed bead, rethread needle back through all beads except for final seed bead. Take a stitch, knotting thread on inside of pillow cover. Take a stitch across inside of cover and exit ⅜" away along the lower edge of the silver trim. Thread beads onto the needle in the order shown in the illustration to make the second length of fringe (the shorter length). Continue as for the first length of fringe, knotting off on the inside and taking a stitch ⅜" over along the edge of the trim. Continue adding lengths of fringe, alternating between the long and short lengths, until you reach the side seam on the opposite side of the pillow. Knot thread and trim thread tails.

Longer fringe

Shorter fringe

6. Insert pillow form into pillow cover. Slipstitch opening closed.

Materials
(for beaded tassel pillow)

- ⅝ yard of silk taffeta
- ⅝ yard of flannel
- 4 silver beads, 7 x 10 mm
- One 4" vial of size 6 blue seed beads
- 1 package of silver-lined crystal bugle beads, 2 x 7 mm
- 1 package of size 11 silver-lined crystal seed beads
- Gray beading thread and beading needle
- 16" square pillow form
- General sewing supplies:
  - Sewing machine
  - Iron and ironing board
  - Rotary cutter, ruler, and self-healing cutting mat
  - Marking pencil
  - Scissors
  - Straight pins
  - Hand-sewing needle

Instructions

1. Press fabrics. Cut two 17" squares from silk taffeta and two from flannel. Layer flannel squares over wrong sides of silk squares. Baste layers together ⅜" from raw edges.

2. Mark points along the edges of the layered fabric squares, ¼" and 3" from corners. Align ruler with ¼" mark on one side of fabric and 3" mark on adjacent side of fabric. Trim, using rotary cutter. Repeat on each side of each corner to taper corners slightly. Repeat on remaining layered fabric square.

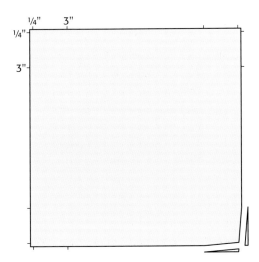

3. Pin silk taffeta squares, right sides together. Stitch ½" from raw edges, leaving an opening for turning. Trim corners. Turn cover right side out; press.

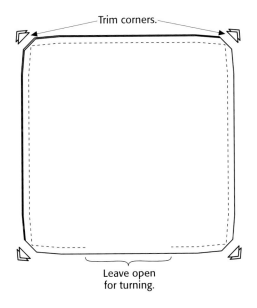

4. Thread beading needle with single strand of beading thread, about 30" long. Insert needle through beads as shown. At bottom seed bead, stop and rethread needle back through all but the bottom seed bead, leaving long thread tails at the top. Repeat to make a total of 24 tassel pieces. Thread the ends of 6 of the tassel pieces into a large silver bead and then a small blue bead, using a needle if necessary, to make one tassel.

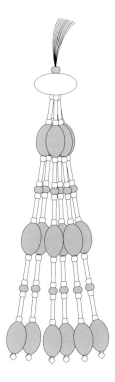

Thread all the thread tails (12) into a large darning needle and take a stitch into pillow at corner. On inside, take a stitch into seam allowance and knot ends to secure tassel in place. Repeat at remaining three corners of pillow cover.

5. Insert pillow form into pillow cover. Slipstitch opening closed.

A plain wooden frame is converted into a beautiful accent piece when covered with a rich brocade fabric, velvet ribbon edging, and iridescent amber glass seed beads. For easy beading, the frame dimensions are marked off on the fabric and the fabric is beaded first; then the fabric is glued to the wooden frame, which is first layered with two pieces of thin batting to provide a smooth and slightly padded surface. Ribbon covers the raw edges of the fabric on the inside and outside edges of the frame. You will need ribbons with widths to match the depth of the frame at the inner and outer edges. When looking for a fabric to cover your frame, select one that has definite lines in the pattern that can be used as a guide for placement of your beads. This brocade had paisley-type motifs that were easy to outline with beads. I also added beads to the centers of some flowers.

Brocade Frame

By Bridget Haugh

Materials

- Frame for a 3½" x 5" photo (6½" x 8½" outside dimensions)
- ⅜ yard of brocade fabric
- ⅜ yard of fusible knit interfacing
- ⅜ yard of thin batting
- 1 yard of velvet ribbon, ½" wide (or depth of frame on outside)
- ⅝ yard of velvet ribbon, ¼" wide (or depth of frame on inside)
- One to two 4" vials of seed beads to coordinate with fabric
- Scissors
- Ruler
- Iron and ironing board
- Straight pins
- Double-stick tape
- Hand-sewing needle
- Thread that contrasts with fabric
- Gold beading thread and beading needle
- Pencil
- Newspaper
- Aerosol adhesive
- Kraft paper
- Pencil or chalk pencil
- X-acto knife
- Tacky glue
- Toothpicks

Instructions

1. Place brocade face up over frame and center design on frame. Mark outer edges of frame roughly on fabric with pins. Cut out fabric, about 3" larger than the frame on all sides. Cut a piece

of interfacing to the same dimensions as brocade rectangle and fuse to the wrong side of the brocade, following the manufacturer's directions.

2. Position fabric back over front of frame and center design; temporarily secure with double-stick tape. Using sewing needle and contrasting thread, stitch around the outer and inner edges of the frame with long stitches. Remove fabric from frame.

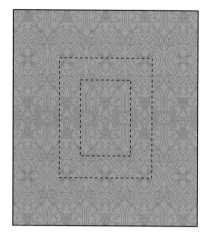

Mark frame dimensions onto fabric
with contrasting thread.

3. Look over the frame fabric and determine which pattern lines in the fabric you want to accent with beads. Choose design lines that will produce even bead distribution across the entire frame. Using beading needle and single strand of beading thread about 18" long, stitch beads onto fabric, following the determined design lines within the marked frame lines (I sewed my beads about ¼" apart). Knot thread at the beginning and end of each length.

4. Trace the frame onto a piece of batting and cut out. Cut a second piece of batting ⅛" larger than first piece on all sides, including the inside area where the photo will go. Cover work surface with newspaper. Cover a second work surface with kraft paper. Place the two batting rectangles on the newspaper and spray with aerosol adhesive. Place the frame, right side up, on the kraft paper. Carefully lift the smaller rectangle of batting; turn

batting over and place on top of the frame. Smooth across frame with hand. Center the second rectangle of batting on top, wrapping the excess around the inner edges and sides.

5. Measure the depth of the frame and mark this distance out from the outer edges of the outer marked thread line on the fabric, using a pencil or chalk pencil. Trim fabric along the outer marked pencil lines. Do not trim away fabric from interior of frame yet.

6. Place fabric over frame using thread marks as a guide for placement. Glue fabric to frame, working from center of each side out to the corners. The fabric will not quite cover the sides of the frame all the way to the back edge due to the depth of the batting.

7. Fold and glue the excess fabric at corners straight down along the side edges of the frame. Trim away the point, if necessary. Allow glue to dry.

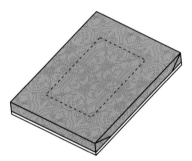

Glue fabric to frame.

8. Working from the back side of the frame, cut an **X** through the center of the frame, clipping almost to the corners. Pull fabric over the inner edge of the frame on one side and secure with glue, trimming away excess fabric. Clip fabric into the corners only as much as necessary to create a smooth fit. Repeat along the remaining inner edges of the frame. Allow to dry; then trim excess fabric with an X-acto knife.

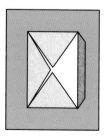

9. Starting at the center bottom of the frame, glue the wide velvet ribbon around the outer edges of the frame, aligning one long edge with back edge of frame and leaving 1" unglued at the ends. Apply glue sparingly to keep it from seeping through the velvet. At the end, overlap ribbon; then trim through both layers at an angle with scissors and remove loose ends. Glue angled ends in place. Cover the raw fabric edges at the inner edge of the frame in the same manner, starting and ending at the top center of the frame. Apply additional glue around the edges of the ribbons if necessary, using a toothpick for a secure hold all the way to the edge of the ribbon.

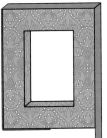

Glue velvet ribbon to inner and outer edges of frame along sides.

This lampshade could easily become a focal point in a room where light reflecting off the glass beads casts a warm glow on the room. It is easily made by stringing beads onto spool wire and wrapping the beaded wire around a ready-made lampshade frame. For additional interest and to help conceal the lower edge of the lampshade frame, beaded dangles are added around the lower edge. They can be subtle or made more dramatic with the use of large beads as shown here. The upper edge of the lampshade is given a softer look with loosely wrapped strands of beads that crisscross back and forth. This project was made with large beads (size 6 seed beads), which helps reduce the time needed to complete the project. For the most interesting look, select an assortment of opaque, transparent, and foil-lined beads to make the project.

Amber Lampshade
By Tracy Stanley

Materials

- Wire lampshade frame (3" diameter at top, 4" height and 5" diameter at base)
- About 300-g size 6 seed beads
- About 80 assorted accent beads of various sizes for embellishment at top and for dangles
- 24-gauge brass or copper spool wire
- 20-gauge copper spool wire
- Six ½" copper jump rings
- Shallow plastic container
- Wire cutters
- Chain-nose pliers
- Round-nose pliers

Instructions

1. Cut a 3-yard length of wire. Wrap one end several times around the top rim and one side rib of the wire lampshade frame. Be careful not to let your wire become tangled. Make a slight curve in the remaining end of the wire.

2. Pour about ⅓ of your seed beads into your plastic container and mix well. Tilt your container slightly and begin scooping the wire into the pile of beads. As the beads begin to line up on the wire, push them down to the end. If you have trouble getting the beads onto the wire, adjust the curve at the end.

3. When you have approximately 1' of beads on the wire, begin to wind the beaded wire around the top rim of the lampshade frame, pushing the rows of beads together for a snug fit. There will be a gap in the beading where the side ribs of the frame are attached to the upper rim. This will be

concealed later. Thread more beads onto the wire as necessary to completely wrap the entire upper rim of the lampshade frame. At the end, wrap the wire three or four times around the top of the frame, pulling tight. Use your chain-nose pliers to help pull it snug and trim off the excess wire.

4. Turn the lampshade frame upside down. Cut a 4-yard length of wire. Attach the wire to a side rib and the bottom rim in the same manner as before. Thread beads onto the wire and wrap the bottom rim of the lampshade frame in the same manner as the top rim of the frame.

5. Cut a 3-yard length of wire. Secure to one rib of the frame next to the top rim with 3 or 4 wraps. Wrap the wire so it passes over the top of the ribs around the shade in the direction you intend to bead. Add some more beads to your plastic container and scoop them onto your wire as before. Line up enough beads to reach the next rib in the shade; there should be enough beads to cover both ribs and the distance between them.

6. For the first wrap, use one hand to hold the beads in place over the first rib while using the second hand to carry the wire over and around the next rib. This will prevent the wire from slipping off the first rib while you are pulling on it. Pull snug for a tight fit. Continue adding beads onto the wire until you have enough to string across and

cover the next rib. Wrap the wire around the next rib and continue in the same manner until you come within two ribs of running out of wire.

7. Cut another 3-yard length of wire and attach to the rib where you plan to end. Be sure to wind it on so the wire passes over the top of the rib. Continue adding beads onto your first wire and continue wrapping the beaded wire around the frame as before until you reach the new wire. Wrap the end of the first wire over the wraps of the newly added wire to help secure it in place. Trim excess from first wire. Add beads to the new wire until you have enough to reach and cover the next rib. As in the beginning, hold your hand over the start point of the new wire as you make your wrap around the next rib. Continue adding beads to the wire and wrapping in the same manner until you reach the end of the frame. Wrap the end of the wire three to four times around a rib at the bottom of the frame and trim excess.

8. To embellish the top of the frame, attach a 3-yard length of wire to the top rim of the frame. Add seed beads and accent beads in any combination for about 1½" or so. Make a test wrap around the upper rim in a diagonal fashion to see if the length fits around the rim. Make the wrap loose. Add or subtract beads as desired. Wrap the wire under the rim and back to the front side of the shade and add more seed beads and accent beads as desired. Push down so the wire is completely covered. Continue to make loose wraps of beads around the upper rim of the frame in the same direction.

When you reach the end, go back in the opposite direction in the same manner, creating a crisscross design around the top of your lampshade.

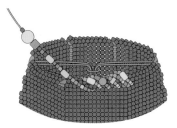

9. Open your jump rings and add them to the lower rim of the lampshade at each rib to help conceal the exposed frame. Cut a 7" length of 20-gauge copper wire. Hold the wire in the jaws of the chain-nose pliers and bend at a 90° angle 2" from one end. Grasp the short end of the wire in the tip of the round-nose pliers, so the long end of the wire extends straight out and parallel to the jaws of the pliers. With your finger, push the short wire around the pliers until it makes a complete circle. Remove the round-nose pliers. Grasp the circle in the jaws of the chain-nose pliers so the long wire is facing down and perpendicular to the pliers. Gently push the wire around the circle with your thumb to make a coil. Remove and reposition tool about every ⅛" to achieve the smoothest looking coil. When you have two complete wraps, trim excess wire, angling cutter for a smooth transition. Now you have a head pin with a coil at the end.

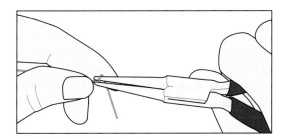

Push wire around pliers to make a circle.

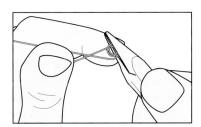

Coil wire around center loop, holding coil with chain-nose pliers.

10. Thread six to eight assorted accent and seed beads onto the head pin. At the end, bend wire at 90° angle, and then wrap the excess wire around one side of the round-nose pliers to make a loop about ¼" above the beads. Wrap the excess wire about 3 times around the ¼" length between the loop and the beads. Trim excess. Repeat to make a total of six dangles.

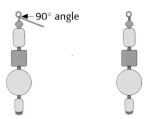

Wrap excess wire 3 times in space between loop and bead.

11. If you want to use a drop bead on the end of your dangles, you will not be able to use a head pin as just described. Instead, cut a 7" length of wire and wrap around one side of the round-nose pliers to make a loop about 2" from one end. Separate the wires without distorting the loop and slide your drop bead onto the wire until it hangs from the loop. Using your chain-nose pliers, bend long wire at 90° angle to loop, and then wrap short wire three times around long wire and trim excess. Thread six to eight beads onto the remaining end of the wire, and then end with a loop in the same manner as for the dangles in step 10.

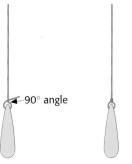

Make loop. Slide bead onto loop and bend long wire at 90° angle.

Wrap short end of wire around long wire 3 times and trim excess.

Thread beads onto remaining end of wire and make loop at end.

12. Open the jump rings, using your chain-nose pliers to rotate half of the ring forward. Insert the loop from the dangle on the jump ring and close the jump ring.

Create this Turkish-style table runner for a rich and elegant look on a dining table. For maximum impact with little hand beading, the runner was embellished with prebeaded appliqués and fringe. For added richness, the runner also features rows of velvet and corduroy ribbon in two different shades of red. The hand-beaded Turkish design created with seed beads was accomplished simply by tacking down every third bead along a prestrung length.

Turkish Table Runner

By Kelley Taylor

Materials

- 2 yards of burgundy fabric (I used crushed nylon)
- Two 18-g vials of size 11 transparent red seed beads
- One 17-g vial of silver-lined dark red pony beads
- 1 yard of 1¼"-long beaded fringe trim with heading
- 1 yard of 2"-long beaded fringe with heading
- 1 yard of 25-mm burgundy corduroy ribbon (Mokuba)
- 1⅞ yards of ¼"-wide deep red velvet ribbon
- Thread to match fabric
- Beading thread and beading needle
- Fabric adhesive
- General sewing supplies:
  - Sewing machine
  - Iron and ironing board
  - Rotary cutter, ruler, and self-healing cutting mat
  - Scissors
  - Straight pins
  - Hand-sewing needle
  - Air-soluble fabric marking pen
  - Wooden hoop
  - Light box
  - Flexible measuring tape
  - Low tack tape

Instructions

1. Cut two 18" x 72" rectangles from fabric. Cut each length of beaded trim in half. Pin the heading of the shorter fringe to one short end of one fabric rectangle, right sides together, with fringe hanging down over the fabric. Cut off excess trim on ends. Using a zipper foot, baste the trim to the end of the table runner. Repeat on the opposite short end of the runner. Stitch the long beaded fringe to the runner over the short fringe in the same manner, taking care to assure that the fringe alternates between short and long lengths if possible.

Baste fringe to end
of table runner.

2. Using an air-soluble marking pen, draw lines across the short end of the runner ¼", 3⅝", and 4⅞" above the fringe stitching line. Repeat on the other end of the runner. Cut the ribbons in half. Cut the narrow

velvet ribbon in half again. Align the lower edge of one corduroy ribbon to the marked line 3⅝" above the fringe and glue in place. Align the lower edge of one velvet ribbon to the marked line 4⅞" above the fringe and glue in place. Trim excess at sides of runner. Repeat on the opposite side of the runner. Reserve the final two pieces of velvet ribbon for step 10.

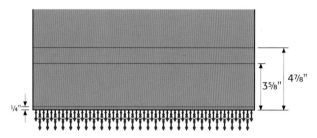

Mark ribbon and beading placement lines.

3. Pin table runner top and bottom pieces, right sides together, keeping beaded fringe away from edges. Stitch ½" from raw edges on long sides and just inside previous stitching on short sides, using zipper foot as necessary and leaving approximately 8" open for turning. Trim corners and turn table runner right side out, carefully pushing out corners. Press with iron, and then slipstitch opening closed.

4. Find the center of the runner width by folding long edges in half; mark the center on the lower marked line. Photocopy or trace the pattern on page 35 onto paper. Tape the pattern to a light box and align the marked center of the fabric with the pattern center, making sure the placement line of the pattern rests on your drawn line; trace pattern.

5. To trace pattern again on both sides of center design, measure and mark ¼" from side edges of marked design. Reposition fabric over pattern, aligning one side of pattern at lower edge with marked point to the side of the first marked design. Trace pattern onto fabric. Repeat on the other side of the center motif. Mark design on opposite end of runner in the same manner.

6. Cut a 36" length of beading thread. String 18" of seed beads onto the thread with beading needle. Remove needle. Tape the ends of the thread to your work surface, to prevent beads from falling off. Repeat to string a total of twelve 12" lengths of beads, leaving needle in last length of beads and wrapping the other end of the thread in tape.

7. Thread beading needle into fabric along lower marked line at the start of the design. Knot end in area below lower marked line and remove needle.

Slide beads down thread and shape along outer marked design line. Tape taut to fabric, just beyond top peak in design as shown below. Thread a second needle with 26" of beading thread. Take a stitch and knot in fabric at the start of the design, next to the beads. Take a stitch through fabric, along the design line, three beads away from the starting point. Pull needle out of fabric and take a stitch across beads to secure and insert needle back into the same hole. Take another stitch through the fabric, pulling needle out three beads away. Take a stitch across beads to secure and insert needle back into same hole. Repeat in the same manner to secure the beads to the marked line. When you reach the top peak in the design, readjust your beaded length of thread so it continues along the marked design line. Tape taut. Continue beading until you reach the marked line ¼" above the beaded fringe. Take a stitch through fabric below marked line, knot, and trim excess. Remove tape and any excess beads that fall below the marked line on the remaining length of thread. Thread the end into the beading needle, take a stitch in the fabric below the marked line, knot thread, and trim excess. Repeat couching process along second pattern line to secure beads in place. At inside corners, it may be necessary to couch in place after each bead rather than after every three beads to maintain the pattern. Repeat beading process for all remaining motifs.

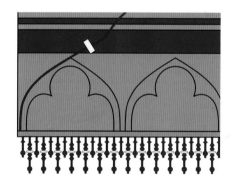

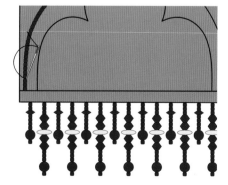

Take a stitch across every third bead
to secure them in place along the design line.

8. Randomly attach single pony beads to fabric as desired in between outer edge of beaded pattern and corduroy ribbon.

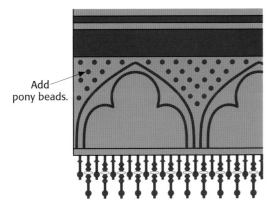

9. Cut six appliqué designs from beaded lace yardage. Pin one to the top arc of each beaded motif and hand tack in place.

10. Glue one of the remaining lengths of velvet ribbon to the lower edge of the runner, concealing any knots. Trim ends ¼" from sides of runner, turn under edges and glue in place. Repeat at the opposite end of the runner.

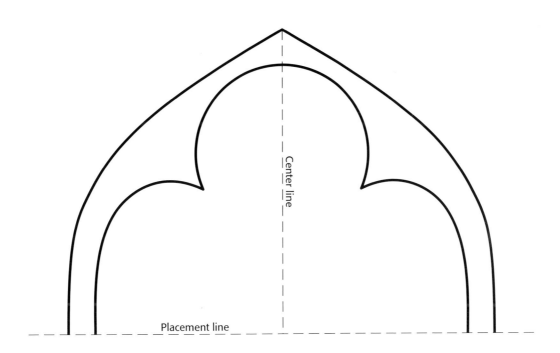

Turkish Table Runner Pattern

These unique ornaments, which showcase silver-lined seed beads, coiled brass spirals, and beaded drops, will add lots of sparkle to your holiday tree. To make the ornaments you need to construct a wire framework that can be wrapped with wired lengths of seed beads. Constructing the framework is a little awkward, but well worth the effort. The beading itself goes rather quickly. I chose to make the frame for the ornaments with brass rods as they are both inexpensive and harder to bend than standard craft wire and therefore make a sturdy frame that does not easily bend out of shape.

Holiday Ornaments

By Dawn Anderson

Materials

(for each ornament)

- 2 hanks of red or gold silver-lined size 11 seed beads
- 1 size .045 round brass rod, 36" long for oblong red ornament (2 rods for gold ornament with pointed tip)
- 28-gauge brass spool wire
- 24-gauge brass spool wire
- 2 size 6 seed beads
- Two 11-mm accent beads
- 9" of gold cording for hanger (with cording diameter small enough to pass through accent bead twice)
- Eye pin from 20-gauge wire
- Head pin from 20-gauge wire
- Wire cutter
- Permanent marker
- Flat-nose pliers
- Round-nose pliers
- Chain-nose pliers
- Masking tape
- Flexible tape measure
- Light-colored flannel or wool scrap (about 14" square)

Instructions

1. Cut three pieces of brass rod, measuring 12" each for oblong ornament or 13" each for ornament with pointed tip, using wire cutter. Mark points on rods at centers, using permanent marker. Hold rod firmly in flat-nose pliers next to marked point. Push rod forward against tool, using thumb to make a 90° angle. Move flat-nose pliers down rod about ½" and continue to push other half of rod forward, stopping before shape of side begins to distort; crimp folded end between jaws of pliers to make a hairpin shape. Repeat bending process for remaining two pieces of rod.

2. Make a small loop at one end of brass rod using round-nose pliers. Remove round-nose pliers; then hold loop in jaws of chain-nose pliers. Begin coiling brass rod around loop by pressing wire away from you using your thumb; keep an even amount of space between the rings of the coil. Open pliers and move along length of wire in about ⅛" to ¼" increments while coiling. Continue coiling until coil measures about ⅜" in diameter. Repeat to make coils at both ends of each frame piece.

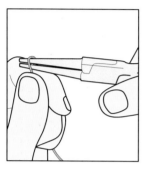 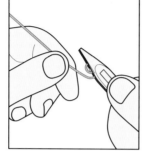

Make loop with round-nose pliers.

Coil wire around center loop, holding coil with chain-nose pliers.

Bend curve in each half of brass rod to match either the oblong or pointed ornament pattern pieces on page 41 by running rod between thumb and forefinger, bending shape into rod with thumb. Bend shape in sides of one piece to match pattern A and bend shape in sides of two pieces to match pattern B; several small movements make a smoother curve than trying to create the shape using a single movement.

3. Cut a 20" length of 24-gauge wire. Place B frame pieces flat on work surface with points at center and coils at ends. Bind together at center with three wraps of 24-gauge wire. Twist ends together securely for about ⅜" and trim off excess on short end with wire cutter. Using thumb and forefinger, bend arc in B frame pieces as shown. Final shaping will be done in step 5. Butt coils at bottom of B pieces, turning coils outward if necessary and using flat-nose pliers. Fold 9" length of cording for hanger in half, wrap under center of B pieces and tie together in knot next to end. Position frame piece A between the attached B pieces, aligning the coiled ends of piece A just above the centers of the B pieces. Position cording hanger between coils of the A piece. Using the chain-nose pliers, bend the piece of 24-gauge wire at a 90° angle ⅜" above centers of B pieces. Hold 24-gauge

wire flat against the A frame piece and wrap wire around the two spokes of the A frame piece for about ⅜" or until the centers of the B frame pieces are not visible. Finish wrapping by making two wraps around a single brass rod; trim off excess. Bend the B frame pieces so that they curve outward, matching the curve in the A frame piece. Adjust the spokes of the frame so there is even space between each. Crimp wrapped wire at top of ornament frame lightly between jaws of chain-nose pliers to flatten slightly.

Bind B pieces together at center.

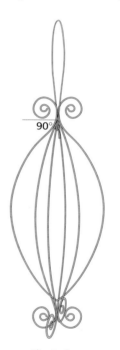 

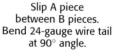

Slip A piece between B pieces. Bend 24-gauge wire tail at 90° angle.

Wrap wire around coiled A pieces to secure frame together at top.

4. Cut a 20" length of 24-gauge wire, and wrap around center bottom of frame piece A; twist ends together securely for about ⅜" and trim off short end of wire with wire cutter. Using chain-nose pliers, bend length of 24-gauge wire at right angle ⅜" from center of frame A piece. Trim eye pin to a length of about 1¼", using wire cutter; cup hand around wire cutter while cutting to catch loose piece and prevent it from flying into the air.

Position eye pin at bottom of ornament, with loop of eye even with coils of frame B pieces, and remaining length of wire projecting up into the center of the ornament frame. Holding eye in place, wrap wire tail around the four spokes of the frame B pieces just above the coils for about ⅜". Finish by wrapping wire twice around one spoke; trim off excess wire with wire cutter. Insert round-nose pliers into center of frame, near bottom; bend small loop at end of eye pin, and coil until wire can be coiled no further to prevent it from slipping through the bottom of frame. Using chain-nose pliers, separate coils at base of frame so that there is equal distance between each.

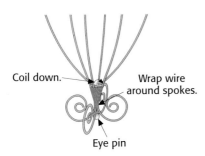

Coil down.

Wrap wire around spokes.

Eye pin

5. Shape sides of frame pieces as necessary between thumb and fore-finger to make shape of each rod identical for a symmetrical look. Wrap tape measure around widest part of frame, and divide distance by 6; record measurement (about 1⅛"). Mark a 9" piece of masking tape with marks spaced the recorded distance apart. Wrap marked masking tape around frame, plac-ing a spoke at each mark-ing on tape until all spokes are positioned evenly apart; overlap tape at ends.

Align spokes of frame with marks on masking tape.

6. Lay flannel or wool scrap on work surface to prevent loose beads from rolling. Cut about 30" of 28-gauge wire. Crimp at one end to prevent beads from coming off. Separate string of seed beads

from hank without removing it from the hank. Starting at one end of string, thread wire through beads a couple inches at a time, so beads are tem-porarily threaded through both the string and the wire. Upon reaching remaining end, push wire 2" past last bead on string then holding tightly to the wire end, remove string from hank and transferred beads. Repeat to transfer all but two strings of beads to wire.

7. Cut a 26" length of wire and wrap end three times around one brass spoke of frame at top of frame. Wrap the wire so it passes over the top of the spokes around the frame in the direction you intend to bead. String two or three beads on wire and wrap wire once around next spoke; last bead should sit on top of spoke. Add two or three more beads and wrap wire once around next spoke. Continue this process, adding additional beads as necessary between spokes until you near end of wire. End by wrapping wire once around spoke and removing any excess beads. Wrap end of a new length of beaded wire around same spoke. Twist ends tightly together with chain-nose pliers and clip twisted ends to ⅜" long using wire cutter. Push twisted ends to inside of ornament. Wrap beaded wire around brass frame. At spokes, spread beads to expose wire, then wrap once around spoke. Continue beading in this manner joining additional lengths of beaded wire as necessary until you reach the bottom of the frame.

8. At the end, it may become difficult to insert the wire around a spoke of the frame. If this happens, thread wire to opposite side of ornament, wrap around any spoke to anchor it, and then insert wire back to opposite side and continue in the same manner until you reach the wire wrapping at the bottom. It is okay to skip a spoke occasionally on the last row or two if there is not room to insert the wire in around the spoke. Finish by threading wire back and forth through frame at bottom and wrapping wire around spokes between the last couple rows of beading until secure. Trim excess wire with wire cutter.

Designer's Tip

For easier retrieval of wire once inserted into the frame at the base of the ornament, make a small curve in end of wire before inserting. This way the end naturally curves back to the outside of the frame and you can grab it and pull the wire through using your chain-nose pliers.

9. Cut a 4" piece of 28-gauge wire and fold in half; crimp at fold to make hairpin shape. Insert center of ornament hanger into center of hairpin shape. Thread ends of wire hairpin through one size 6 seed bead and one 11-mm accent bead and pull beads down to upper edges of coils. Clamp end of coil at top of ornament in jaws of chain-nose pliers and bend coil downward to make additional space for beads at top. Repeat on other side. Push beads as close to top of ornament as possible.

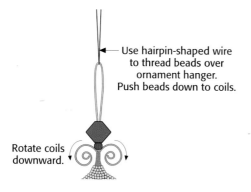

Use hairpin-shaped wire to thread beads over ornament hanger. Push beads down to coils.

Rotate coils downward.

10. Insert head pin into size 6 seed bead and then one 11-mm accent bead. Trim excess wire about a scant ⅜" above accent bead, using wire cutter. Grasp wire in jaws of round-nose pliers near tip and roll forward to make a loop. Remove round-nose pliers and grab base of loop along longest length of wire with chain-nose pliers. Rotate hand back, bending loop at a sharp angle. Remove pliers and reinsert round-nose pliers into loop; rotate forward to make a complete circle and make the beaded drop.

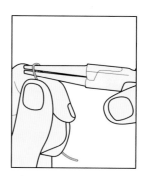 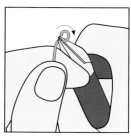

Rotate back at sharp angle.

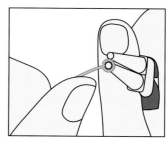

11. Open eye by grasping one half in the jaws of chain-nose pliers and rotating it away from you. Do not pull eye apart to open or you will distort the round shape of the eye. Slip end of open eye onto wire loop at bottom of ornament and close eye. To close eye, grasp half of eye in chain-nose pliers and rotate it to a closed position; continue to rotate past the closed position until it opens again and then rotate back to a closed position to help set the shape.

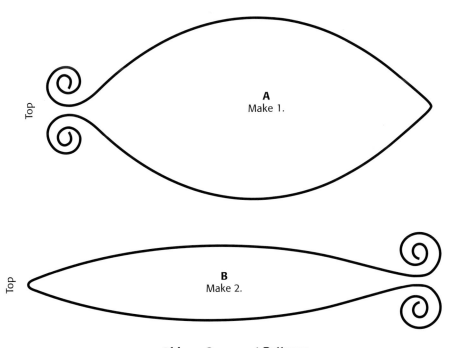

A
Make 1.

Top

B
Make 2.

Top

Oblong Ornament Patterns

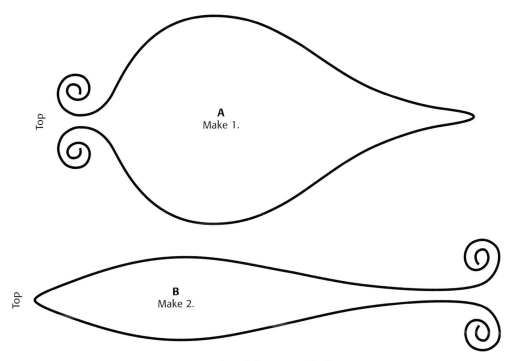

A
Make 1.

Top

B
Make 2.

Top

Pointed Ornament Patterns

This delicate place mat and coaster set are constructed by simply wrapping a continuous length of beaded wire around the center again and again until the desired size is achieved. Each row is secured to the previous row using anchor wires that radiate out from the center of the circle, like spokes on a bicycle wheel. The edging is completed on the same wire by counting off a predetermined number of beads and twisting at set intervals to make the circular pattern.

Circular Place Mat and Coaster

By Elizabeth Cameron

Materials
(for one 15" place mat with 11" center and one 6" coaster with 4" center)

- 7 hanks of size 11 seed beads (transparent medium dark aqua from Shipwreck Beads; see "Sources" on page 80)
- 28-gauge silver spool wire
- 34-gauge silver spool wire
- Scissors
- Chain-nose pliers
- Wire cutters
- Ruler
- Tape

DESIGNER'S TIP

To make the napkin ring shown, select 8 to 10 beads about 10 to 14 mm long. Following steps 1–3 on pages 49–50 for the Crystal-Draped Chandelier, insert 18-gauge wire through each bead and make a loop on each end, and then connect the beads to make a circle about 2" in diameter.

Instructions
(for 1 place mat)

1. Prepare a 3" piece of tape and stick it within easy reach at the edge of your work surface. Arrange loops of beads in the first hank so that one end of each 20" string of beads is contained in your left hand and the other end of each strand is contained in your right. Being careful to prevent any beads from slipping from the strands, snip the knot containing all strand ends. Lay the ends contained in your right hand at the top edge of your work surface and secure them there with tape. Push the beads up against the tape barrier at the top end of each strand and carefully lay the "left-hand" strand ends down flat on the work surface.

2. Unspool several feet of 28-gauge wire, but do not cut it. Separate one string of seed beads from others taped to work surface. Separate free end of string and thread wire through beads a couple inches at a time, so beads are temporarily threaded onto both the string and the wire. Upon reaching taped end, push wire 2" past last bead on string. Then, holding tightly to the wire end, remove string from transferred beads. Repeat for each strand in six hanks, unwinding more wire and

sliding the strung beads further down the wire as necessary. (Each hank will yield approximately 20' of beaded wire.)

3. Leave a wire tail approximately 15" long. To temporarily secure the beads strung on the wire, fold the free end back toward the beaded portion of the wire, forming a loop. Twist the wires at the base of the loop several times to form a solid barrier for the strung beads. Moving from the "looped end" toward the "spool end," eliminate any gaps by sliding all the beads toward the looped end. Clip the wire from the spool 1" past the last strung bead. To permanently secure the last bead on the spool end of the beaded wire, wrap the wire around the outside of the last bead and back through the hole, pulling it through with the chain-nose pliers. Trim the excess.

Insert wire around and through last bead to secure; clip excess.

4. Grasping the "permanently secured" end of the beaded wire in the chain-nose pliers, form a tight coil of beads. Release the center bead after two revolutions of the pliers. (The beaded wire will uncoil slightly but retain the general shape that will form the center of the place mat.)

5. Cut four 13" lengths of 34-gauge wire and fold each length loosely in half. Secure the first complete ring of beads to next concentric ring with one length of the 34-gauge wire. Slide one half of the folded wire beneath the inner beaded circle. Nestling the 34-gauge wire between second and third beads, form an X with the two ends of the "anchor wire" by pulling one end up into the air above the work surface and pushing the other end to be flush with the work surface. Position the portion of the beaded wire that completes the next concentric ring into the V created by the ends of the anchor wire attached to the inner ring. (One half of the anchor wire will travel beneath each newly added ring, while the other travels above it. The rings are secured in place by alternating placement of each half of the anchor wire between the top and bottom positions.)

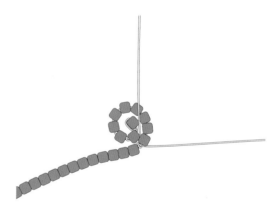

Crisscross wire to make an "X" across beads and secure ring of beads in place.

6. Use the remaining lengths of 34-gauge wire to form equidistant "anchor spokes." Repeat the "crisscross" maneuver with the ends of the anchor wire for each pass of the beaded wire to enlarge the central portion of the mat. When you reach the point where the anchor spokes are 1" apart, add an additional spoke between each original spoke, for a total of eight spokes. Continue winding the beaded wire around the growing center portion, anchoring it at each spoke location, until the beaded center has a diameter of 11". (Add additional spokes when the ends of the eight anchor spokes are 1" apart.)

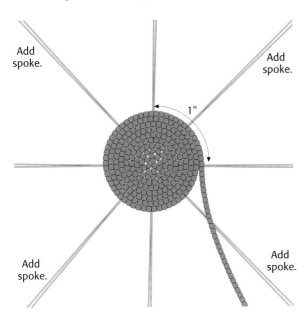

Add spoke.

Add spoke.

Add spoke.

Add spoke.

1"

When the beading distance between spokes equals 1", add additional spokes to the outer ring, centered between original spokes.

7. Create space on the beaded wire by undoing the loop at the wire's end. Re-create a much smaller loop at the end to keep beads from sliding off the end of the wire, and slide all remaining beads toward the loop. (The edgework is completed on the same beaded wire that has formed the center solid section, but the repetitive twisting requires that the beads not be packed snugly on the wire.) To form the first "double loop" for the edging, slide 58 beads up to the last anchor spoke location for the center section. Form a single large loop by folding the wire holding the 58 beads in half and twisting the two endpoints together. Divide the single large loop into the desired double loop shape by counting off 18 pairs of beads (one half of each pair on each wire ascending from the twist at the base) and performing a second twist. Plump the resulting oblong shapes into rounded circles.

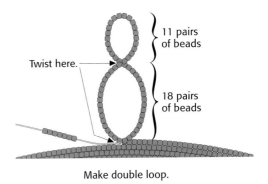

11 pairs of beads

Twist here.

18 pairs of beads

Make double loop.

Shape circles.

8. To form the first "triple loop" (and allow the required space between the looped elements), slide 106 beads up the wire until they are flush with the first looped element. Count off 18 beads to act as a uniform spacer between looped elements; then form a large single loop with the remaining 88 beads. Perform a second twist after 11 pairs of beads (starting from the base twist) to form the first small circle. Count up 22 pairs of beads from the second twist and perform a third twist to create the large middle circle and a second small top circle (which by default contains 11 pairs of beads). Shape the beads into three circles.

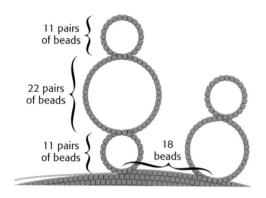

9. To form the second "double loop," slide 76 beads up the wire until they are flush with the first triple looped element. Count off 18 beads to act as a uniform spacer between looped elements; then form a large single loop with the remaining 58 beads. Divide the single large loop into two smaller loops by counting off 18 pairs of beads (starting at the base twist) and performing a second twist. Shape into two circles.

10. Continue alternating double and triple loop elements until the edgework wire nearly encircles the perimeter of the solid center section. Anchor the base wire (containing the 18-bead spacer segments) to the solid center with the anchor spokes. Assess the remaining distance from the last looped element to the first looped element to determine how many additional looped elements are necessary. If necessary, adjust the standard 18-bead spacer segments between future looped elements to evenly distribute the remaining edgework. Include enough beads on the final spac-er (after the last looped element) to reach to the base of the first beaded element. Clip the wire 1" past the last bead on the spacer segment. To permanently secure the last bead on the beaded wire, pass the wire once again through the last bead. Pull the end through the bead hole with chain-nose pliers; then clip the end of the wire flush with the bead. Use the anchor spoke at the first beaded element to secure the end of the wire to the body of the place mat.

11. Twist the two ends of each anchor spoke wire around one another several times, trim the wires ¼" from last crisscross over beaded edgework wire and tuck the ends underneath the place mat.

Instructions
(for 1 coaster)

1. Follow steps 1 to 5 above for the place mat, using only 1 hank of beads. Use the remaining lengths of 34-gauge wire to form equidistant "anchor spokes." Repeat the "crisscross" maneuver with the ends of the anchor wire for each pass of the beaded wire to enlarge the central portion of the coaster to 4".

2. Create space on the beaded wire by undoing the loop at the wire's end. Re-create a much smaller loop at the end to keep beads from sliding off the end of the wire, and slide all remaining beads toward the loop. (The edgework is completed on the same beaded wire that has formed the center solid section, but the repetitive twisting requires that the beads not be packed snugly on the wire.) To form the first "double loop" for the edging, slide 58 beads up to the last anchor location for the center section. Form a single large loop by folding the wire holding the 58 beads in half and twisting the two endpoints together. Divide the single large loop into the desired double loop shape by counting off 18 pairs of beads (one half of each pair on each wire ascending from the twist at the base) and performing a second twist. Plump the resulting oblong shapes into rounded circles as on page 45 in step 7 for the place mat.

3. To form the first "single loop" (and allow the required space between the looped elements), slide 40 beads up the wire until they are flush with the first double-looped element. Count off 18 beads to act as a uniform spacer between looped elements; then form a small single loop with the remaining 22 beads.

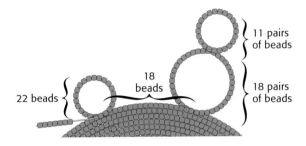

22 beads

18 beads

11 pairs of beads

18 pairs of beads

DESIGNER'S TIP

To help de-emphasize the anchor spokes, use a fingernail or a dull-edged blade (such as a letter opener) to gently push the spoke wire down toward the work surface between each concentric row of beads. (Performing this action periodically during the creation of the center section of the mat also helps prevent the spoke wires from becoming too tight, which can cause the giant circle to "pucker" or look scalloped.)

4. Continue alternating between double and single looped elements as in step 10 for the place mat. Finish the coaster as in step 11 for the place mat.

Create a dramatic display with swags of sapphire and crystal beads and sapphire teardrops draped from a chandelier. The faceted beads I used glisten in the light for added effect. I used a candle chandelier here, but this would also work on a dining room light fixture that has five arms. Only a few simple techniques are needed to create this eye-catching accent. Since I had a black fixture, I used black wire to create the eye loops on my beads. If you have a silver- or gold- toned fixture, you may want to substitute a matching wire, using a size that is as close as possible to the gauge wire listed below.

Crystal-Draped Chandelier

By Dawn Anderson

Materials

- 1 package (100 g) of 19-gauge black craft wire (Darice)
- 1 package (85 g) of 22-gauge black craft wire (Darice)
- 150 light sapphire blue fire-polished round beads, 10 mm
- 81 sapphire blue fire-polished round beads, 10 mm
- 40 crystal fire-polished round beads, 10 mm
- 5 light sapphire blue teardrop crystals (The Antique Lamp Co., see "Sources" on page 80)
- Wire cutter
- Round-nose pliers
- Chain-nose pliers
- Flat-nose pliers
- ¼"-diameter mandrel, such as a knitting needle or nail
- Chandelier

Instructions

1. Cut a 1½" length of 22-gauge wire. Grasp wire in jaws of round-nose pliers near tip and roll forward (away from you) to make a loop. Remove round-nose pliers and grab base of loop along longest length of wire with chain-nose pliers. Rotate hand back (toward you), bending loop at a sharp angle. Remove pliers and reinsert round-nose pliers into loop as far as it will go; rotate forward to make a complete circle with a stem that is centered exactly under the circle. You have just created an eye pin.

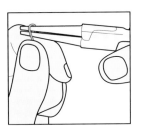 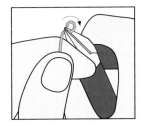

Rotate back at sharp angle.

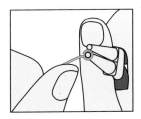

2. Thread a bead onto remaining end, trim wire to about a scant ⅜" and make another loop in the same manner. Cut more wire and add to remaining beads, making a loop at each end.

Make 150 light sapphire blue.   Make 81 sapphire blue.   Make 40 crystal.

3. Join beads as shown below to make five outer swags and five inner swags. See "Designer's Tip" on page 52 and add or subtract beads from the swags as necessary to fit your chandelier. To join beads, hold bead and grasp half of one eye in jaws of chain-nose pliers and rotate hand forward. Do not pull eye apart from the side as that will distort the round shape. Slip end of open eye onto wire loop of a second bead and close eye. Close eye in the same manner in which you opened it, rotating back to a closed position.

Outer Swag
Make 5.

Inner Swag
Make 5.

4. Grasp wire end of teardrop crystal in round-nose pliers and rotate pliers to coil up wire, making a double loop. Join six beads and a teardrop crystal as shown.

Make 5.

5. To make the support for the beaded swags, cut a 15" length of 19-gauge wire. Wrap the wire twice around the mandrel at the center and twist ends once to secure, then pull ends out at a 90° angle. Remove from mandrel. Center the double loop on the outside of the chandelier just under the candleholder. Wrap the ends around to the inside and twist together for ½"; trim excess and press end flat against the chandelier. Repeat at the remaining four arms of the chandelier.

Make double loop.

Twist ends together, trim excess, and press flat against chandelier.

6. Cut a 15" length of 19-gauge wire and wrap twice around the mandrel a couple inches from one end; then twist ends once to secure. Remove from mandrel. Center the double loop under the candleholder on the inside of the chandelier, at the point where the chandelier arms are attached to the candleholder support. Wrap the longer end of the wire around the outside of the chandelier and back to the inside. Make a couple wraps around the base of the double loop and trim excess wire.

Twist excess wire around base of loop.

7. Measure the distance between the chandelier arms at the center support of the chandelier where the arms meet, and record measurement. Cut a length of 19-gauge wire about twice the circumference of the support. Make five double loops in the wire spaced the recorded distance apart. Wrap wire with double loops around the upper edge of the interior center support of the chandelier and twist ends together for ½". Trim excess and press end flat or push into center of chandelier.

Measure the distance between arms.

Make five double loops in wire a measured distance apart.

Wrap wire around interior support.

8. Wrap 22-gauge wire snugly 15 times around mandrel to make a coil. Remove from mandrel and pull coil apart so there is some space between the rings. Trim end flush. Then trim apart the rings to make 15 jump rings, making a flush cut on each end of the wire. Open jump ring as for eye hole on beads and join one to each double loop on chandelier.

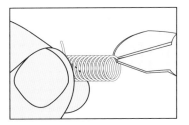

Trim rings of coil apart to make jump rings.

Make 15 jump rings.

9. Join outer swags to chandelier by connecting loops of end beads to jump rings at outside of each chandelier arm. Join the loop of the end bead on the crystal teardrop piece to the jump ring on the outside of each chandelier arm.

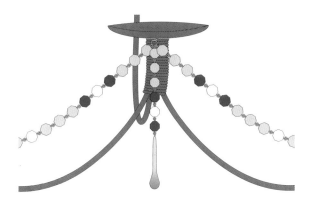

10. Join inner swags to chandelier by connecting end loops of swags to jump rings at inside of each chandelier arm and to the jump rings at the interior center support of the chandelier. On this chandelier, the center support wire is placed higher then the support wire on the inside arms so the swag end that finishes with four sapphire beads was connected to the center and the swag end that finishes with two sapphire beads was connected to the inner arm support. This allows the center design to hang in the center of the swag.

11. To make the crystal drop at the center, wrap a 20" piece of 19-gauge wire once around the center loop of the chandelier and twist once to secure. Place the mandrel directly below the center loop and wrap one end of the wire around it; then make a couple wraps around the previous twist. Trim ends and remove mandrel. Join a sapphire bead to a teardrop crystal; then join the remaining loop on the bead to wire loop at the center bottom of the chandelier.

DESIGNER'S TIP

All light fixtures vary in their construction. As long as you can easily wrap wire around the arms under the light or candleholder and around the center in some way, you should be able to drape it with beads. You can also decorate a chandelier that has three, four, or six arms as well. The bead order I used here allows for a repeated series of beads that falls in the center of each swag (two medium sapphire, one crystal, and two medium sapphire). When attaching your beads together, take this into consideration and add equal numbers of beads to each side of a center pattern. Then test fit the swag to see if the center pattern falls in the center. If the attachment point at the interior center support of your fixture is higher or lower than the attachment point at the inside arms, you may need to add or subtract beads from one side or the other for the center pattern to fall in the center of the swag. On my chandelier, the attachment point at the interior center support is higher than the attachment point at the inside arms, therefore my beaded swag ends with four sapphire beads at the center support and two sapphire beads at the inside arm support.

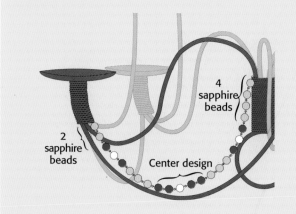

2 sapphire beads

4 sapphire beads

Center design

Apply simple beading techniques to a wire mesh shade to create beautiful floral designs that sparkle in candlelight. The floral clusters of beads are all done in silver to create a wonderful monochromatic look against the silver wire mesh. Although the beading may look intricate or difficult, upon further inspection you will find that this project requires only adding beads and twisting wires. When the floral clusters or center stems are broken down step by step, you will see how easy and quick they are to create.

Wire Mesh Candle Shade

By Genevieve A. Sterbenz

Materials

- ½ yard of 36"-wide aluminum wire mesh, 30 x 30 denier
- 30-gauge silver spool wire
- 24-gauge silver spool wire
- 2 packages of 4-mm quartz beads
- 1 package of 3-mm silver beads
- 1 package of 6-mm crystal teardrops
- 1 hank of size 11 silver-lined crystal seed beads
- 1 package of 5-mm flat silver floral-shaped spacers
- 1 hank of size 2 (2 x 4.5 mm) straight silver-lined crystal bugle beads
- 1 package of 9-mm silver bead caps
- 1 package of 6-mm flat silver spacers
- 1 package of 4-mm silver beads
- 1 package of 9-mm silver teardrops
- 1 package of silver tubular spacer beads with slight curve, 2 x 27 mm (Elite Better Beads, Hirschberg Schultz & Co.)
- 1 package of flat crystal rhinestones in assorted sizes
- Four 1.5-cm dragonfly charms
- Rectangular frosted candle hurricane shade, 3¼" x 3¼" x 5" tall

- 5" x 5" silver candle plate (optional)
- Ruler
- Black marker
- Scissors
- Work gloves
- ⅛"-wide masking tape
- Wire cutters
- Fun-Tak reusable adhesive putty
- Chain-nose pliers
- 2 small wooden blocks
- Fabri-Tac Permanent Adhesive (see "Sources" on page 80)

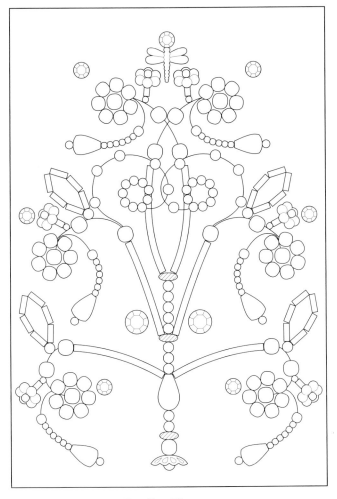

Beading Diagram

Instructions

1. Measure, mark, and cut one 14½" x 5½" rectangle from wire mesh, using ruler, marker, and scissors. Wear work gloves while cutting. Place rectangle in horizontal position on work surface. Fold down a ¼" hem on two opposite long sides using ruler and straight lines of mesh weave to guide you. Fold down a ¼" hem on two opposite short sides in same manner. Measure and mark three vertical lines, 3½", 7", and 10½" from the left side. Turn mesh over to right side and place rectangle in horizontal position once again. Measure and mark three vertical lines, 3½", 7", and 10½" from the left edge, using straight edge of ruler and ⅛"-wide masking tape. Set mesh aside.

2. To make individual quartz flowers, start by cutting a 10" piece of 30-gauge wire. Thread one quartz bead onto the wire and slide bead to midpoint. Bend wire in half and twist wires together a couple times right below bead. Thread seven more quartz beads onto both wires. Leave about ⅛" between the first bead and the remaining seven beads. Loop wire with seven beads around in a circle and twist ends around the ⅛" space. Bend single bead into the center of the circle leaving the two wires outstretched. Twist wires together for ¼".

Add 7 beads to both wires.

Form circle and twist ends together.

Bend single bead into center of circle.

3. To add the two accent beads, slide one quartz bead onto only one wire and slide it up as far as you can. Twist both wires at base of bead. Add another quartz bead ¼" from the last bead. Do not cut wires. Set aside.

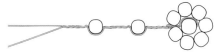

Make 6.

4. Measure and cut three 4" pieces of 30-gauge wire. Set two pieces of wire aside. On one piece of wire, slide one 3-mm silver bead to midpoint. Fold wire in half and twist at base of bead. Add one crystal teardrop through both wires, widest part of bead first, followed by six seed beads. Then add one 3-mm silver bead to one of the wires and slide it up to the base of the seed beads. Twist both wires at the base of the silver bead to secure and complete a teardrop flower bud. Do not cut wires. Set aside. On second piece of wire, slide one seed bead to the midpoint. Fold wire in half and twist at base of bead. Add one 5-mm flat floral spacer, followed by a bugle bead. Add one seed bead to one wire, slide it up to the bugle bead, and twist both wires at the base to complete a small flower. Do not cut wires. Set aside. On third piece of wire, slide six bugle beads to the center of the wire. Bring both ends together and twist wires. Bend wire in half so that there are three bugle beads on each side. Slide one 3-mm pearl onto one wire. Slide it up under the bugle beads and twist wires at its base to complete a bugle-bead leaf. Do not cut wires. Set aside.

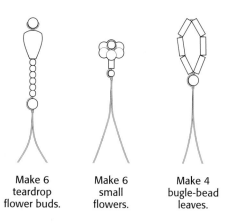

Make 6 teardrop flower buds.　　Make 6 small flowers.　　Make 4 bugle-bead leaves.

5. To assemble a floral cluster, place quartz flower stem on work surface. At base of flower, add the teardrop flower bud by twisting the wires together. Trim crystal teardrop wires only, leaving flower wires long and intact. Add the small flower in the same manner at the base of the flower. Trim those wires only. Add the bugle-bead leaf above the quartz bead closest to the wire ends by twisting the wires together. Trim the wires on the leaf piece only to complete one floral cluster. Make five more floral clusters in the same manner as the first one, except on two clusters omit the beaded "leaf." Set all six clusters aside.

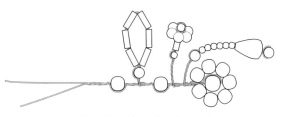

Make 6 (4 with leaf and 2 without).

6. Measure and cut three 20" lengths of 30-gauge wire. Gather three wires together and slide one 4-mm silver bead to midpoint of all three. Bend wires in half, bringing ends together. Add one bead cap, threading all six wires through it. Then thread on one quartz bead, one 6-mm flat silver spacer, two 4-mm silver beads, and one 9-mm silver teardrop. Separate two wires from the bunch, so that 4 remain together in the center. Bend the fifth wire out to the right and the sixth to the left.

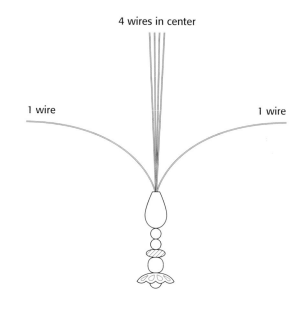

4 wires in center

1 wire　　　　　　　　　　　　1 wire

7. Add a tubular silver bead to each of the out-stretched wires, positioning it so the curve arches outward. Place the wires of one flower cluster (with the beaded leaf) into the tubular bead. Then wrap the wire running through the tubular bead around the base of the flower cluster, and then a couple wraps up the stem of the cluster (placing the wire under any beads) to secure it in place. Trim away any excess wire.

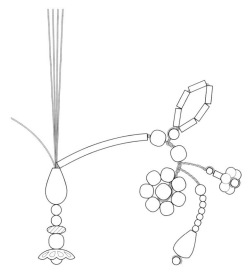

Place flower cluster in tube.
Use wire from tube to wrap
around the cluster.

8. Add a flower cluster on the opposite side. Thread all four remaining center wires through three 4-mm silver beads and one 6-mm flat silver spacer. Separate the wires again so that two remain in the center. Bend the third and fourth wire out to the right and left sides. Add a tubular silver bead to each outstretched wire, positioning it so the curve arches outward. Add two more flower clusters (with the beaded leaves) to the silver tubes as before. Change the cluster slightly by bending the crystal teardrop piece around the other side of the flower as shown in the beading diagram on page 55.

9. Thread both remaining wires through four 4-mm silver beads and a 6-mm flat spacer. Add a tubular silver bead to each of the outstretched wires, positioning it so the curve arches inward. Add the last two flower clusters (each without the beaded leaf) as shown in the beading diagram on page 55. Set aside.

10. Measure and cut a 10" piece of 30-gauge wire. Slide nine 3-mm silver beads to midpoint of wire. Bring both ends together to form a circle of beads and twist wire at base for 3/8". Separate the two wires and add one 3-mm silver bead onto one wire. Slide up as far as it will go and twist wires to secure. Twist wires for another 3/8" and add a second 3-mm silver bead. Continue in this manner, adding three more beads (five total). Twist ends for 3/8". Curve beaded wire around as shown in diagram to make the top section of half of a heart. Set aside. Repeat these steps to make the top of the second half of the heart. Secure one of the heart sections to the design by twisting the wire stem to the wire stem of the middle flower cluster, just above the tubular bead. Trim away excess wire. Repeat to secure the second heart piece on the remaining middle flower cluster.

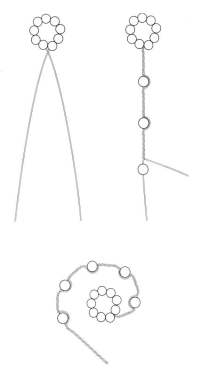

11. Place mesh shade horizontally on work surface, right side up, hem side down. On one panel (area between strips of masking tape), center beaded stem and flower clusters. Temporarily secure in place with small pieces of Fun-Tak. Arrange beads as shown in the diagram. Interlock the heart sections along the curve between the first and second silver beads after the circle of silver beads. Measure and cut ten 2" pieces of 30-gauge wire.

At center, thread one small piece of wire from back side of mesh through hole to front side. Wrap around center stem of beads, through mesh again, and out the back side. Use chain-nose pliers to help insert wire into mesh. Twist wire ends together on back to secure, using chain-nose pliers. Do not snip excess wire off just yet. Continue to secure beaded design to mesh in the same manner. When everything is in place, remove Fun-Tak and snip excess wires on back side of mesh. Press ends flat against mesh along a design line to conceal. Position dragonfly charm at the center top of the design as shown in the diagram on page 55 and secure with wire. Raise top edge of mesh off work surface by placing small wooden blocks under the top two corners. Using glue, attach nine rhinestones, following diagram. Allow glue to dry.

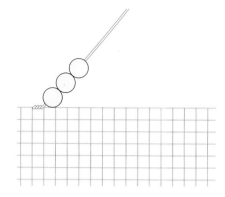

12. Repeat steps 2 through 11 for the remaining three panels of the shade. To create the shade, turn wire mesh to wrong side and place in a horizontal position. Place ruler along first marked line and gently fold the mesh up against the edge of the ruler to create a 90° angle. Repeat with remaining two marked lines. Stand shade upright.

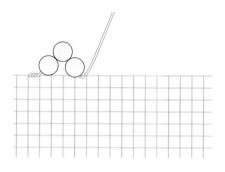

13. To create the top beaded border, measure and cut a 20" piece of 24-gauge wire. At top left edge of first panel of shade, thread wire from backside around to front and back through a few times in the same place to secure that one end of the wire in place. Working at the upper edge of the shade, bring free wire end to front side of shade. String three 4-mm silver beads onto wire. Bring wire up and over the top of the shade and insert through upper edge of mesh to the backside about ¼" away. String one quartz bead onto wire. Bring wire up and over the top of the shade, and then insert into the mesh to the back side, one bead length away. Continue adding a group of silver beads followed by a quartz bead in this manner until the entire upper edge of mesh is embellished with beaded edging. Wrap wire around mesh at top right side to finish and secure.

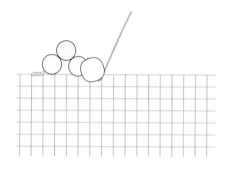

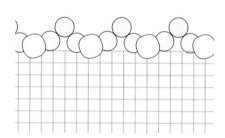

14. To create the seed bead looped edging, measure and cut a 45" piece of 24-gauge wire. Create small loop at one end and twist to secure. This will keep beads from falling off the wire. String all but 3" of the wire with seed beads. Create small loop and twist at remaining end of wire. Begin at one end of wire and measure out 1¼" of beaded wire. Using your thumb and forefinger to mark the measurement, make a loop from the 1¼" length of beaded wire. Cross wires when they meet and twist twice. Count out six seed beads. Use your thumb and forefinger to hold the six beads in place; then measure out 1¼" along the beaded wire. Use your thumb and forefinger on the opposite hand to mark this measurement and bend only these beads into a loop. Cross wires at the beginning and end of the 1¼" length and twist loop once. Continue in this same manner until 36" of looped beaded wire is completed. To make loops round, push a marker through the holes. Make two.

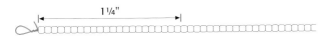

Make loop and twist.

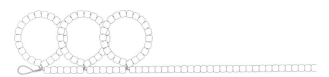

Count 6 beads and loop.

15. To attach the seed bead looped edging to the bottom edge of the shade, open shade and place on work surface. Do not push down on mesh and distort existing folds. At the lower left edge of shade, line up end of beaded edging. Using a 26" length of 30-gauge wire, lash the beaded edging to the shade, along the entire lower edge. At the right edge, trim the beaded edging to fit (trim slightly longer, remove excess beads, and twist end around shade to secure). Add looped edging to the upper edge of the mesh shade in the same manner, positioning it just behind the existing edging. To add beaded accents to bottom edge, leave shade in this position. Measure and cut 16" of the 30-gauge wire. Crimp one end of wire to keep beads from sliding off. String three 4-mm pearls and one quartz bead onto the wire. Continue to add three pearls and one quartz bead until 14" has been strung with beads. Crimp other end of wire. Using ten 2" pieces of the 30-gauge wire, secure one end of the wired beads to the bottom left edge of the shade, just above the looped edging. Continue to attach beaded wire to the entire lower edge of the shade using the 2" pieces of wire.

16. Stand shade up and wrap it around the frosted glass hurricane shade. Line up the edges where the two ends of the mesh shade meet. Use the 16" of 30-gauge wire to lash the edges of the shade together. Take a couple stitches through mesh at ends to secure. Trim excess.

Create a sparkling glass bead cover to transform an ordinary drinking glass into a beautiful flower vase. To create the cover, I first built a wire frame from 14-gauge wire. Then I wrapped beads, threaded onto wire, around the frame, securing them around each vertical support. I used small seed beads, which are inexpensive, to cover the largest portion of vase. I added four rows of larger accent beads around the top to create a border and one row of accent beads at the bottom to balance the design. I coiled the ends of the vertical wire supports for added interest around the top of the vase. Because the beads add extra width to the design, I chose a drinking glass that was somewhat narrow to end up with a tall slender vase. This technique can be applied to a variety of glass containers as long as the bottom of the glass is equal to or smaller in diameter than the opening at the top and the sides of the glass are straight or angle outward slightly at the top. This allows for easy removal of the glass container for cleaning.

Sparkling Vase

By Dawn Anderson

Materials

- Glass (about 2" base diameter x 6¼" tall x 3" upper rim diameter)
- 8' of 14-gauge sterling silver or silver permanent-colored copper wire
- 28-gauge silver spool wire
- 10" of 24-gauge silver spool wire
- 4 hanks of size 11 pink seed beads
- About 184 accent beads (I used 5.5-mm Saturn Beads)
- Flexible tape measure

- Wire cutters
- Permanent marker
- Flat-nose pliers
- Round-nose pliers
- Chain-nose pliers
- Soup can
- Masking tape
- Light-colored flannel or wool scrap (about 14" square)

Instructions

1. Use a wire cutter to cut four pieces of 14-gauge wire measuring 22" each, using a wire cutter. Set aside excess; it will not be needed for this project.

2. Mark center of each 22" length with permanent marker. Then mark points 1⅛" to each side of center marks. Hold wire firmly in flat-nose pliers next to outer marked point. Push rod forward (away from you) against tool, using thumb to make a right angle at marked point. Repeat at second outer marked point on rod to form a staple shape. Bend wire at center mark in the same manner to create a 45° angle as shown. Repeat for the remaining lengths of wire to make the sections of the wire frame.

Center
1⅛" 1⅛"

45°

Make 4.

3. Use round-nose pliers to make a small loop at one end of one wire frame piece using round-nose pliers. Coil the loop away from the 45° angle. Remove round-nose pliers; then hold loop in jaws of chain-nose pliers. Begin coiling wire around loop by pressing wire away from you using thumb;

keep an even amount of space between the rings of the coil. Open pliers and move along length of wire in about ¼" increments while coiling. Continue coiling until coil measures about ⅝" in diameter. Repeat to make coils at both ends of each frame piece.

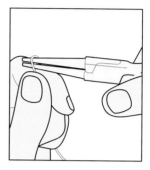

Make loop with round-nose pliers.

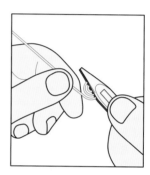

Coil wire around center loop, holding coil with chain-nose pliers.

4. Place frame section against glass and shape frame to fit. Use flat-nose pliers to angle sides outward slightly at base, if necessary. Add slight curve in sides near top by running wire between thumb and forefinger, bending shape into rod with thumb. Several small movements make a smoother curve than trying to create the shape using a single movement. Shape each section of the frame the same.

5. Place glass upside down over soup can. Position two frame sections around the glass, so the midpoints are aligned on the bottom of the glass. Bind the frame pieces neatly together at the center bottom of the glass, using 24-gauge wire and leaving ¹⁄₁₆" between the midpoints. Do not cut wire.

Position the remaining two wire frame sections around the glass to make an eight-spoked design. Bind the remaining two frame sections together at the midpoints. Remove frame from glass and twist ends of binding wire together to one side of the wrapped area, using chain-nose pliers. Trim twisted wire to ¼" and fold end over to the inside. Crimp flat with flat-nose pliers.

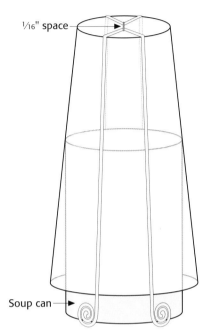

1/16" space

Soup can

Bind 2 frame sections together.

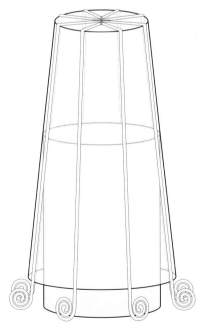

Bind remaining 2 frame sections to first 2.

6. Wrap masking tape around base of glass and around rim at upper edge. Measure glass circumference at base and top and divide into eight equal segments using permanent marker to make tick marks. Marks at top should align with marks at bottom. Position glass back over soup can with wire frame on top, aligning each spoke of frame with tick marks. Lift frame about ½" above the glass and tape spokes in place.

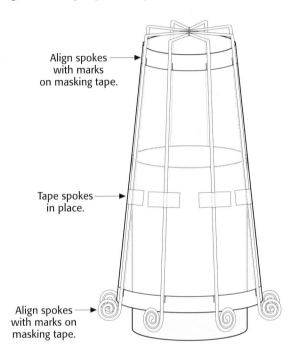

Align spokes with marks on masking tape.

Tape spokes in place.

Align spokes with marks on masking tape.

7. Lay flannel or wool scrap on work surface to prevent loose beads from rolling. Cut about 40" of 28-gauge wire; crimp at one end to prevent beads from coming off. Separate string of seed beads from hank without removing it from the hank. Starting at one end of string, thread wire through beads a couple inches at a time, so beads are temporarily threaded through both the string and the wire. Upon reaching remaining end, push wire 2" past last bead on string. Then holding tightly to wire end, remove string from hank and transferred beads. Repeat with remaining strings to make about a 30" length. Make about three small loops at end. Repeat to transfer all but two strings of beads to wire. Cut strings on remaining beads and slide off onto flannel.

8. Cut a 26" length of wire and wrap end three times around one wire spoke of frame at center bottom, so wire comes over top of frame in the direction you intend to bead. String two beads on wire and wrap wire once around next spoke. Add two beads to wire and wrap wire once around next spoke. Continue adding beads in this way to make one circle around bottom of frame. Continue to add beads to wire and wrap around spokes of frame, allowing a bead to sit on top of each spoke.

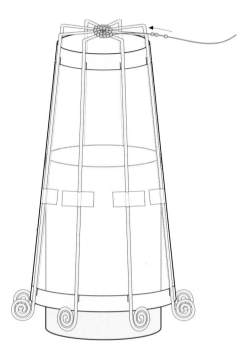

9. Continue wrapping beads around spokes in the same manner until you reach end of wire. End by wrapping wire once around spoke and removing any excess beads. Wrap end of a new length of beaded wire around same spoke. Twist ends of wire tightly together with chain-nose pliers and clip twisted ends to ⅜" long using wire cutter. Press twisted end against wire frame on inside.

Continue beading in the same manner until the entire base is beaded. When the base is nearly finished, check to see that the wire frame extends evenly around all edges of the beaded area. If it is uneven, straighten the wire with the flat-nose pliers and readjust angles as necessary for the base to be symmetrical. Continue beading if necessary until entire bottom of frame is covered with beads.

10. Remove excess seed beads from the wire you are beading with. Add accent beads to wire, alternating with a seed bead until you reach the next spoke of the frame. If you reach the next spoke and it hits in the middle of an accent bead, remove the bead and determine how many seed beads can be added in order to reach the next spoke. If necessary remove beads just added and rearrange so that accent beads fall evenly between the two wire spokes, with seed beads filling in any gaps on each side. Thread beads in the same sequence between the next two spokes. Continue in the same manner until 1 row of accent beads is added. Then continue to add a couple rows of seed beads, joining lengths together as necessary.

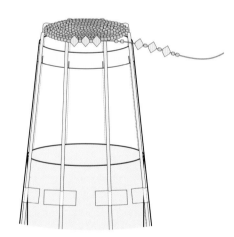

Add row of accent beads
(using same sequence of beads)
between every pair of spokes.

11. Remove tape holding frame to glass. Set frame upright and place glass inside, align frame spokes to tick marks, and check fit. If too snug, remove a couple rows of beads and readjust. Continue adding rows of seed beads around frame, checking after every couple rows to be sure frame still fits snugly around glass and spokes are aligned with tick marks.

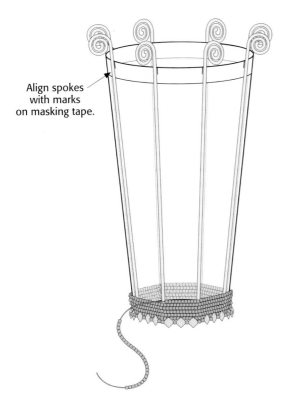

Align spokes with marks on masking tape.

12. Bead until you reach about 2" from top of coils (beaded design will take up about 1½"). End around a spoke and remove excess seed beads from wire. To the beading wire, add alternating seed beads and accent beads as before, taking care to space accent beads evenly between spokes. Use extra seed beads at spokes if necessary. Make one complete row of accent beads, then three rows of seed beads. Continue in this manner two more times; then finish with a row of accent beads. At end, wrap wire tightly back down spoke, threading through rows of wires as necessary for about 1"; then trim excess. If coils are too high, continue coiling them down or shape outward to desired position. If not tall enough to allow room for the last rows of beads, uncoil slightly.

1½"

Add beaded border, alternating rows of accent beads with 3 rows of seed beads.

These delicate candle wreaths add interest to plain glass candleholders. The larger wreath is made by stringing beads onto lengths of wire to resemble vines, which are then intertwined to make the wreath. For the small candle wreaths, I made a wire ring to fit the candleholder and then wrapped the ring with beads. Twisted wires with small flowers, leaves, and berries extend out from the base of the wreaths, producing a wispy appearance.

Floral Candle Wreaths

By Dawn Anderson

Materials
(for pillar candle wreath)

- 3" x 3" pillar candle and desired candleholder
- 1 bag (1,200 count) of size 11 iridescent medium orchid seed beads (Cartwright's, see "Sources" on page 80)
- Two 6" vials of size 11 silver-lined celery green seed beads
- 102 crackled orchid 4-mm beads for buds
- 14 crackled orchid 6-mm beads for flower centers
- 14 lime 10 x 8-mm leaf beads
- 192 pale yellow 4-mm beads for flower petals
- 28-gauge silver spool wire
- Wire cutters
- Chain-nose pliers

Materials
(for 2 taper candle wreaths)

- 2 taper candles and desired candleholders
- Silver-lined size 11 celery green seed beads (about 200)
- 124 crackled orchid 4-mm beads for buds
- 10 crackled orchid 6-mm beads for flower centers
- 10 lime 10 x 8-mm leaf beads
- 80 pale yellow 4-mm beads for flower petals

- 20" of 16-gauge silver permanent-colored copper wire (Artistic Wire)
- 28-gauge silver spool wire
- Wire cutters
- Chain-nose pliers

Instructions
(for pillar candle wreath)

1. Cut five 70" lengths of wire using wire cutters. Thread a 4-mm orchid bead onto the wire, stopping about 10" from the end. Bend wire around the bead, twisting together in a tight spiral under the bead for about ½" to ¾". Add another 4-mm orchid bead to one wire only; then twist the wires together in a tight spiral under the bead for about ½" to ¾" again. Thread celery seed beads onto long wire tail for 1" to 1¾", pushing beads down to the stop point.

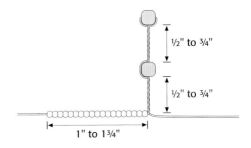

2. Resume bead stringing, adding a pair of 4-mm orchid beads on a twisted wire stem about every 1" to 1¾". Continue for about 8½" to 9", ending with a pair of orchid beads on a stem. Set aside. Repeat process with four additional lengths of wire, mixing medium orchid seed beads with the celery beads on one of the lengths. On two of the lengths, occasionally replace the 4-mm accent bead on the end of a twisted wire stem with a flower and leaf. To do this, thread a 6-mm orchid bead onto the wire, about 2" from the main strand. Bend wire back on itself and twist once to secure. Thread about eight pale yellow beads onto the wire and wrap the strand around the orchid bead to make a complete circle; add more beads or remove some as necessary. Twist to secure. Continue twisting in a tight spiral for about ⅜" to ½". Then thread a leaf bead onto the wire, stopping when the base is about ⅜" to ½" away from the main stem. Bend the wire down the back of the leaf and twist in a tight spiral under the leaf until you reach the main stem. Then make one more twist. Add a 4-mm orchid bead and continue twisting back to the main strand.

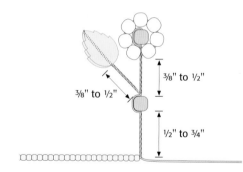

I added these flowers about every 3" along two of my beaded wire strands. Cut a 26" length of wire and bead about 12½" with a mixture of celery and medium orchid seed beads. Coil ends of wire about three times around round-nose pliers to prevent beads from coming off.

3. You should have a total of six bead strands. Add about 2" of seed beads to the ends of all but the 12½" long strand, so the strands vary in length between 12½" and 13¼". Coil ends of wire about three times around round-nose pliers to prevent beads from coming off. Take one strand and uncoil the wire at the end. Insert the end of the wire into the beginning of the strand and the wire end at the beginning into the end of the strand for about ¾" on each side to make a complete circle. Pull wire tails out and add a 4-mm orchid bead to each, stopping about 2" from the main strand. For each, bend wire back on itself and twist in a tight spiral for ½" to ¾", add another 4-mm orchid bead, and continue twisting until wire is twisted all the way back to the main beaded strand. Insert wire ends into holes of six continuous beads along main strand and clip close to exit point as shown.

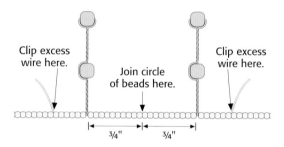

4. Wrap another beaded strand around the first circle of beads, making about three wraps around the circle of beads to give the look of intertwined vines. Join the ends as for the first strand of beads. Repeat with the remaining four strands of beads to make a beaded wreath-like candle collar.

Instructions
(for 1 taper candle wreath)

1. Cut 10" length of 16-gauge wire using wire cutters. Coil wire around twice, so ends overlap slightly, making a circle with about a 5" circumference. Use your fingers to shape the circle. Cut a 70" length of 28-gauge wire. Make about three wraps around wire ring at join to secure temporarily.

2. Place a 4-mm orchid bead on the wire, stopping about 2" from the wire ring. Bend wire around the bead, twisting together in a tight spiral under the bead for about ½" to ¾". Add another 4-mm orchid bead; then twist the wires together in a tight spiral under the bead for about ½" to ¾", until you reach the bottom rim of the wire ring. Thread two celery seed beads onto wire; then add another pair of 4-mm orchid beads on a twisted wire stem. Wrap wire around the outside of ring so that seed beads cover the ring on the outside and the twisted stems rest on the top and bottom rims of the ring.

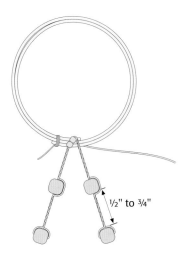

½" to ¾"

Then wrap wire around the inside of the ring, back around to the bottom rim. Continue in the same manner, adding pairs of 4-mm orchid beads on twisted wire stems, separating them with two seed beads on the outside of the wire ring. Stop when a little more than one-third of the ring is covered.

3. Slide beads and stems evenly around ring. Celery seed beads will form a diagonal pattern. Unwrap wire from ring at end and twist ends together using chain-nose pliers. Trim end ⅜" from ring.

4. Cut a 70" length of 28-gauge wire. Wrap a couple times around ring to secure temporarily. Add two celery seed beads; then wrap around ring between previously wrapped beads. Continue in this manner, filling in the gaps. Every inch add a flower and leaf bead on a twisted stem. To do this, thread a 6-mm orchid bead onto the wire, stopping about 2" from the main strand. Bend wire back on itself and twist once to secure. Thread about eight pale yellow beads onto the wire and wrap the strand around the orchid bead to make a complete circle; add more beads or remove some as necessary. Twist to secure. Continue twisting in a tight spiral for about ⅜" to ½". Then thread a leaf bead onto the wire, stopping when the base is about ⅜" to ½" away from the main stem. Bend the wire down the back of the leaf and twist in a tight spiral under the leaf until you reach the main stem; then make one more twist. Add a 4-mm orchid bead and continue twisting back to the main strand. Continue adding pairs of seed beads to fill in the gaps in the diagonal pattern and add a total of five flowers with leaves on twisted stems around the ring. At the end, unwrap the beginning of the wire and join the ends by twisting for ⅜". Trim excess and press end to inside of ring.

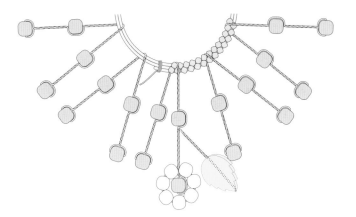

A distressed wire hurricane shade is given a soft, feminine look when embellished with pastel beads and beach glass. Use a "wrap and trap" technique to secure the beads and beach glass to a length of wire, and then wrap the beaded wire around the body of the hurricane shade, securing it in place along the vertical supports with additional lengths of wire. This technique works well on a variety of different wire containers. For best results, match the wire color as closely as possible to the color of the item you are embellishing, or use silver wire, which is neutral in color.

Beach Glass Candle Hurricane Shade

By Elizabeth Cameron

Materials

- About 280 assorted frosted and transparent beads (amethyst, sea green, bottle green, and cerulean blue)
- About 65 pieces of sea glass (½" to ¾" pieces)
- 24-gauge silver spool wire
- 28-gauge silver spool wire
- Wire mesh hurricane shade
- Wire cutters
- Chain-nose pliers

Instructions

1. Cut a 20' length of 24-gauge wire. Unwind 10" of 28-gauge wire from a spool, but do not cut. Hold the two wire ends together and twist the 28-gauge wire around the 24-gauge wire about three times for a spiral about ½" long. Slip the first bead onto the 24-gauge wire and slide it down to the spiraled section. To lock the bead in place, wrap the 28-gauge wire around the 24-gauge wire several times, ending 1" to 1¾" from the bead just added. Repeat the process with three or four additional beads; then add a piece of sea glass. To add the occasional piece of sea glass to the wire containing the beads, use one hand to hold the sea glass firmly in place against the 24-gauge wire (flush with the last twist of 28-gauge wire trapping the last strung bead). Continuing in the same direction as the last bead-trapping twist, wrap the 28-gauge wire around the sea glass several times, in several directions, trapping the 24-gauge wire behind the sea glass with each pass. Use the irregularities in the shape of the sea glass to help secure the wraps of 28-gauge wire in place and prevent it from slipping off. When the sea glass is secure, make one last wrap with the 28-gauge wire that

finishes by wrapping around the free end of the 24-gauge wire. Twist the 28-gauge wire around the 24-gauge wire several times to mimic the pattern between the strung beads.

2. Continue adding beads and sea glass until you reach the end of the 24-gauge wire. Trap the last bead; then spiral the 28-gauge wire around the 24-gauge wire for ½" and clip the wire from the spool. Create a second bead-and-sea-glass-studded wire of the same length.

3. Wind the twined ends of one of the beaded wires around a vertical support at the top rim of the hurricane shade. Cut a length of 28-gauge wire equal to the height of the hurricane, plus 4", for each vertical support. Anchor the 28-gauge wires at the top of each vertical support. Wind the beaded wire around the hurricane shade. Wrap the 28-gauge wire around the vertical supports between the rings of the hurricane, about every inch or so, securing the decorated wire as it passes each vertical support. At the end of the first beaded strand, wind the twined ends around the nearest vertical support, trimming off any excess. Start wrapping the second bead-and-sea-glass wire at the same vertical support. At the base of the hurricane shade, trim the excess beaded wire about 1" from the closest vertical support and wind the twined ends around the support. Wind the end of each 28-gauge wire twice around its respective vertical support, clip the remaining wire, and tuck the end behind the vertical support.

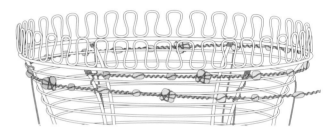

Yellow translucent beads are used to create the forsythia blooms on this stunning pillow. The blooms are strung on wire to help them keep their shape. They are attached to beaded branches made by intertwining lengths of beads strung on wire. First the design was beaded, and then it was tacked onto a ready-made pillow. Choose a pillow with a removable cover to make attaching the beaded design easier.

Forsythia Pillow

By Kelley Taylor

Materials

- One 18" ready-made pillow with removable pillow cover
- One 18-g vial of size 11 brown seed beads
- One 18-g vial of size 11 variegated earth tone seed beads
- Two 18-g vials of size 11 yellow transparent seed beads
- 24-gauge coated brass spool wire
- Shallow dish
- Wire cutters
- Round-nose pliers
- Chain-nose pliers
- Flexible measuring tape
- Straight pins
- Thread to match pillow cover
- Hand-sewing needle

Instructions

1. In a shallow dish, combine the package of brown beads with the package of variegated beads and mix well. Cut a 40" length of wire for the tall forsythia branch in the center of the pillow. String 32" of seed beads onto the wire, crimping wire at ends so beads don't fall off. Set beaded wire aside. Cut two 30" lengths of wire for side branches. String one wire with 23" of beads and the other with 20" of beads. Crimp wire at ends.

2. Fold each beaded wire in half and twist together loosely to make the branches. At the two ends for each branch, bring end of wire around last bead and reinsert it through the same hole. Pull wire end tight, trapping bead in loop. Bend short end at 90° and clip, leaving ⅜" tail. Use round-nose pliers to shape into loop.

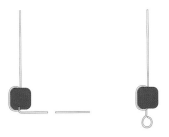

3. Cut 19 pieces of wire, each 15" long, for the forsythia blossoms. Crimp one piece of wire 2" from the end. Thread 2" of yellow beads onto the other end and slide down to the crimped point. Fold beaded section in half and twist ends together a couple times directly under beads to secure and complete one 1"-long petal. Add 2" of yellow beads to the wire. Fold beaded section in half and twist a couple times to complete another petal. Repeat two more times to complete four petals total.

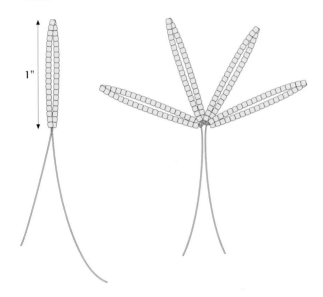

1"

4. Gather the four wired petals together and twist ends of wire together several times to secure. Trim excess wire on short end. Shape petals so they arch outward to complete the forsythia bloom. Make 18 more blooms in the same manner as the first.

Make 19.

5. Wrap wire stem on blossom several times around one of the main twisted beaded branches at one of the points indicated in the beading diagram below. Crimp with chain-nose pliers and trim excess wire. Repeat to secure a total of 12 blossoms to the main twisted branches as shown.

6. On the remaining blossoms, add about 1" to 2" of variegated beads to the wire stem (make two stems measuring 2"). At the end, bring end of wire around bead and reinsert it through the same hole. Pull wire end tight, trapping bead in loop. Attach the 2"-long stems to the main branches first, and then attach the shorter stems to both the main branches and the 2"-long stems as indicated in the diagram. Crimp with pliers and trim excess wire.

7. Remove pillow cover from pillow. Arrange your branches of forsythia as desired and pin in place with safety pins; use the photo and beading diagram as a guide for placement.

8. Using needle and thread, tack branches to pillow cover to secure in place. Remove safety pins. Insert pillow form back into pillow cover and fasten closure on cover.

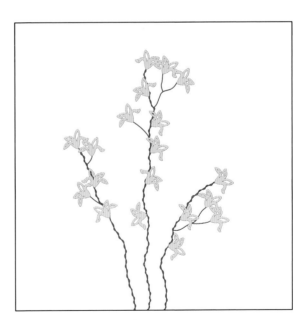

Beading Diagram

The glass seed beads on these votives produce a colorful glow in the candlelight, highlighting the beaded flower and butterfly embellishments. The simple removable beaded sleeves cover most basic glass votive holders. Make a set with flowers, with butterflies, or mix and match the embellishments as shown here.

Butterfly and Flower Votives

By Elizabeth Cameron

Materials
(for a three-votive set)

- 3 glass votives
- Six 18-g vials of size 11 seed beads (two vials each of Lt. Green Lustre, Yellow Lustre, and Topaz-Pink from Blue Moon Beads; see "Sources" on page 80)
- 1 size 6 seed bead in desired color for each of the flower centers
- 28-gauge silver spool wire
- 34-gauge silver spool wire
- Tray or plate to hold loose beads
- Round-nose pliers
- Chain-nose pliers
- Wire cutters

Instructions
(for beaded votive sleeve)

1. Unwind several feet of 28-gauge wire from the spool but do not cut it. Carefully pour one vial of seed beads into a tray or plate. Load the beads onto the wire, unwinding more wire and sliding the strung beads further onto the spool when necessary. String the second vial of the same color bead onto the same wire. (Two vials of size 11 beads will yield approximately 19' of beaded wire.)

2. Leave approximately 4" of wire at the end of the beaded wire. To temporarily secure the beads strung on the wire, fold the free end back toward the beaded portion and form a loop. Twist the wires at the base of the loop to prevent beads from falling off. Moving from the "looped end" toward the "spool end," eliminate any gaps by sliding all the beads toward the looped end. Clip the wire from the spool 1" past the last strung bead. To permanently secure the last bead on the spool end of the beaded wire, wrap the wire around the outside of the last bead and back through the hole, pulling it through with the chain-nose pliers. Trim the excess.

Insert wire around and through last bead to secure; clip excess.

3. Cut four 8" lengths of 34-gauge wire and fold each length loosely in half; set aside. Turn glass votive upside down on work surface. Wrap the finished end (with bead permanently secured) of the beaded wire once around the circumference of the glass votive. (The beaded wire rests flat against the work surface for stability.) Secure the first ring of beads by sliding half of one length of folded 34-gauge wire under the beaded wire. Nestling the "anchor" wire between the second and third beads, form an **X** with the two ends of the "anchor wire"

by pulling one end toward and the other end away from the votive.

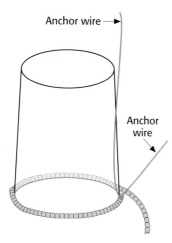

4. Position the portion of the beaded wire which completes the first ring around the votive on top of the first strand into the V created by the ends of the anchor wire. Repeat the X motion with the ends of the anchor wire, trapping the beginning of the second ring of beaded wire snugly on top of the first. Position the three remaining lengths of 34-gauge anchor wire evenly around the first beaded ring, making an X with each to secure to the first ring of seed beads.

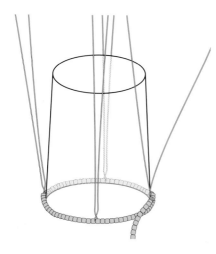

5. Continue wrapping the beaded wire around the votive. At each anchor wire, repeat the X motion to secure the beads in place.

6. When the votive surface has been completely covered by the rings of beaded wire, loosen the loop at the end of the beaded wire, re-create a

smaller loop, and slide all but two beads flush with the looped end. Clip the beaded wire 1" past the two beads extending beyond the last anchor location. Permanently secure the final bead on the wire, circling the votive by wrapping the wire around the outside of the last bead and back through the hole, pulling it through with the chain-nose pliers; then trim the excess. (Secure the end of the wire containing the extra beads with a small temporary loop. Set aside for use in decorative elements.) Twist the two ends of each anchor wire together several times, using chain-nose pliers. Trim the wires to ¼" and tuck the ends between the votive and the beaded sleeve.

7. For each votive, make one or more flowers or butterflies (page 79) for decorative accents. To attach the decorative element to the votive, cut two 2" lengths of 34-gauge wire. Fold each anchor wire in half loosely around the beaded wire at opposite sides of the butterfly or flower, forming an X with each wire beneath the decorative element. Disguise the anchor wire by nestling it between the beads on the decorative element. Carefully slide the beaded sleeve off the bottom end of the votive. Holding the decorative element approximately one inch above the surface where it will be attached, use the chain-nose pliers to insert the ends of each anchor wire between the rows of beads. When all four ends of the anchor wires have been inserted, gently push the decorative element toward the surface of the beaded sleeve. When the flower or butterfly is flush with the beaded surface, use the pliers to reach into the interior of the beaded sleeve, twist each pair of anchor wires together, and clip excess to hold the decorative element securely in place. When all decorative accents have been attached, gently slide the beaded sleeve back onto the glass votive (working from the bottom up).

Butterfly and Flower Embellishments

Instructions
(for 1 butterfly with pink wings and green antennae using leftover beads from votives)

1. Cut two 4" lengths of 28-gauge wire. Using round-nose pliers, make a tiny loop at one end of each wire. Thread four green seed beads onto each wire and slide until snug against the loop. Thread both antennae wires through two consecutive green seed beads to form head. Bend both wires up at right angles to hold beads snug.

2. Thread 20 pink seed beads onto one wire. Form beaded section into a loop and secure by twisting once at base of the head section. Repeat process for second wire. Thread both wires through two green seed beads to form the body section. Bend both wires up at a right angle to hold beads snug. Thread 15 pink seed beads onto one wire. Form beaded section into loop and secure by twisting once at base of body. Repeat process for second wire. Thread both wires through two green seed beads until snug. Clip wires ¼" beyond last bead. Using round-nose pliers, form a tiny loop at the end of each wire to hold beads in place.

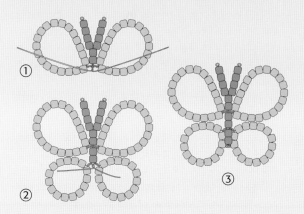

Instructions
(for 1 flower with pink petals and yellow center)

1. Cut a 15" length of 28-gauge wire and make a small temporary loop at one end to keep beads from sliding off. To form the first inner petal, thread 15 pink seed beads onto wire. Form beaded section into a loop and secure by twisting once at the base. Repeat process until five small petals are completed. Unwind temporary loop at end of wire.

Curve wire into tight circle so that two ends of wire can be twisted around one another (and the five petals are spaced equally around the edge of a small center circle).

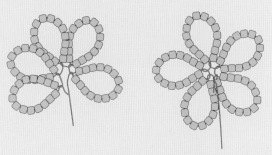

2. To form the first outer petal, thread 20 pink seed beads onto the long end of the wire. Form beaded section into a loop and secure by twisting once at the base. Repeat process until five large petals are completed. Curve petals into tight circle so that the two ends of the wire can be twisted around one another (and the five large petals are spaced equally around the edge of the small center circle, underneath each small petal). Twist ends together for ¼"; trim excess wire. Tuck twisted stem under center section of the flower.

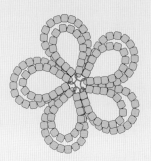

3. To add center, cut a 3" length of 34-gauge wire and fold it loosely in half. Slide one pink seed bead onto wire so it settles in crease. Thread both ends of wire through one yellow size 6 seed bead. Twist wire ends together twice; then separate them at right angles. Position the center beads over the central hole in the petal section. Slide each wire end over opposite edges of the outside ring created by the petals. Pull the wire ends together from underneath the flower, until the center is nestled between the petals and obscures all twisted bases. Twist the loose ends of the wire together to secure it, trim the excess wire, and tuck the twisted end flat beneath the center section.

Sources

The Antique Lamp Co.
1213 Hertel Ave.
Buffalo, NY 14216
716-871-0508
www.antiquelampco.com
Teardrop crystals
(Crystal-Draped Chandelier,
page 49)

Beacon Adhesives
800-865-7238
www.beaconcreates.com
Adhesives
(Floral Lampshade, page 7,
Silk Box, page 13, Turkish
Table Runner, page 33)

Beads and Beyond
25 102nd Ave. NE
Bellevue, WA 98004
425-462-8992
Sterling silver wire and beads
(Sparkling Vase, page 61;
Amber Lampshade, page 29)

Blue Moon Beads
800-377-6715
www.bluemoonbeads.com
Seed and bugle beads
(Forsythia Pillow, page 73;
Turkish Table Runner, page 33;
Butterfly and Flower Votives,
page 77)

**Cartwright's Sequins
and Vintage Buttons**
www.ccartwright.com
sequins@valuelinx.net
Fax 479-369-4213
Seed beads and sequins
(Flower Napkin Ring, page 11)

Shipwreck Beads
2500 Mottman Rd. SW
Olympia, WA 98512
800-950-4232
www.shipwreck-beads.com
Beads
(Circular Place Mat and Coaster,
page 43; Butterfly and Flower
Votives, page 77; Crystal-Draped
Chandelier, page 49)

**Special Shapes
Catalog Division**
PO Box 7487
Romeoville, IL 60446-0487
800-51-4273
Brass rod
(Holiday Ornaments, page 37)

Walnut Hollow
1409 State Road 23
Dodgeville, WI 53533
800-950-5101
www.walnuthollow.com
*Wood boxes, including Classic Box,
Cornice Box, and Recipe Box*
(Silk Box, page 13)